Vulnerability and the Organisation of Academic Labour

Vulnerability theory identifies structural and institutional factors that build or undermine the resilience of individuals and organisations. This volume uses vulnerability theory to explore how the organisation of the teaching and research activities of universities impact the resilience of academics and also how these activities themselves are impacted by contemporary developments in universities and educational policy.

The starting point of enquiry is that neither academics nor universities are invulnerable, and that urgent attention is needed to reverse developments that undermine their resilience. The contributions focus on universities in the US and UK, legal education in the UK, criminal justice in the UK, Brazilian legal education, research in deprived communities, and the ethics of medical professionals. This broad range of subjects is connected by use of vulnerability theory to interrogate academic practices and universities as organisations which should build resilience in their workforce and communities and in so doing secure their own resilience, but which far too often fail to do so, and actually undermine resilience. It is argued this is not due to malefic intentions but to institutional features of the sector and society.

Of immediate interest to anyone who works in, studies at, or relies upon the research mission of universities, and to those involved in the management of universities, this book will also be relevant to policy analysts and policymakers, who will find value in the reframing of vital issues in higher education policy by vulnerability theory, allowing a more realistic and productive policy environment to develop. This book was originally published as a special issue of *The Law Teacher.*

Graham Ferris is a retired associate professor who still teaches legal theory at Nottingham Trent University. He has published on property law, legal history, legal theory, ethics, and legal education. He has three adult children and hopes to continue research using vulnerability theory in the future.

Martha Albertson Fineman is Robet W Woodruff Professor of Law at Emory University. She is the Founding Director of the Vulnerability and the Human Condition Initiative. A Fellow of the American Academy of Arts and Science and recipient of the Ruth Bader Ginsburg Lifetime Achievement Award, she has received numerous awards for her interdisciplinary scholarship on vulnerability, dependency, care, and the legal regulation of intimacy.

Vulnerability and the Organisation of Academic Labour

Edited by
Graham Ferris and
Martha Albertson Fineman

Routledge
Taylor & Francis Group
LONDON AND NEW YORK

First published 2025
by Routledge
4 Park Square, Milton Park, Abingdon, Oxon OX14 4RN

and by Routledge
605 Third Avenue, New York, NY 10158

Routledge is an imprint of the Taylor & Francis Group, an informa business

British Library Cataloguing in Publication Data
A catalogue record for this book is available from the British Library

ISBN13: 978-1-032-77369-8 (hbk)
ISBN13: 978-1-032-77372-8 (pbk)
ISBN13: 978-1-003-48273-4 (ebk)

DOI: 10.4324/9781003482734

Typeset in Myriad Pro
by Newgen Publishing UK

Publisher's Note
The publisher accepts responsibility for any inconsistencies that may have arisen during the conversion of this book from journal articles to book chapters, namely the inclusion of journal terminology.

Contents

Citation Information

The following chapters in this book were originally published in *The Law Teacher*, volume 55, issue 1 (2021). When citing this material, please use the original page numbering for each article, as follows:

Introduction

Introduction
Graham Ferris and Martha Fineman
The Law Teacher, volume 55, issue 1 (2021), pp. 1–4

Chapter 1

Vulnerability theory and higher education
Risa L. Lieberwitz
The Law Teacher, volume 55, issue 1 (2021), pp. 5–23

Chapter 2

Undermining resilience: how the modern UK university manufactures heightened vulnerability in legal academics and what is to be done
Graham Ferris
The Law Teacher, volume 55, issue 1 (2021), pp. 24–41

Chapter 3

Rethinking the neoliberal university: embracing vulnerability in English law schools?
Doug Morrison and Jessica Guth
The Law Teacher, volume 55, issue 1 (2021), pp. 42–56

Chapter 4

Vulnerability, the future of the criminal defence profession, and the implications for teaching and learning
Nicola Harris, Roxanna Dehaghani and Daniel Newman
The Law Teacher, volume 55, issue 1 (2021), pp. 57–67

Chapter 5

Vulnerability theory as a tool against a banking model of legal education
Fabrizia Serafim
The Law Teacher, volume 55, issue 1 (2021), pp. 68–78

Chapter 6

The positive and negative roles of grant funding as mechanisms for societal transformation and the development of community resilience
M. Joan Wilson and W.R. Sexson
The Law Teacher, volume 55, issue 1 (2021), pp. 79–87

Chapter 7

The university's fragile role in fostering societal resilience by facilitating the development of community-engaged professionalism
W.R. Sexson and M.J. Wilson
The Law Teacher, volume 55, issue 1 (2021), pp. 88–100

Notes on Contributors

Roxanna Dehaghani, Cardiff School of Law and Politics, Cardiff University, Cardiff, UK.

Graham Ferris, Associate Professor in Law, Nottingham Law School, Nottingham Trent University, Nottingham, UK.

Martha Albertson Fineman, Robert W. Woodruff Professor of Law, Emory University, Atlanta, Georgia, USA.

Jessica Guth, Leeds Trinity University, Leeds, UK.

Nicola Harris, Cardiff School of Law and Politics, Cardiff University, Cardiff, UK.

Risa L. Lieberwitz, School of Industrial and Labor Relations, Cornell University, Ithaca, New York, USA.

Doug Morrison, Leeds Law School, Leeds Beckett University, Leeds, UK.

Daniel Newman, Cardiff School of Law and Politics, Cardiff University, Cardiff, UK.

Fabrizia Serafim, Emory University, Natal, Brazil.

W.R. Sexson, School of Medicine, Emory University, Atlanta, Georgia, USA.

M. Joan Wilson, Dean's Office, Emory School of Medicine, Emory University, Atlanta, Georgia, USA.

Preface

Some things have remained the same since the publication of the original special edition of *The Law Teacher*. The increase of non-tenured positions in the United States and the United Kingdom, as well as the rise of precarious or contractual labour in both countries continues.[1] The challenges to the traditional consensus around ethical standards governing academics that had served to moderate the relationship between professionalism and educational policies and practices, not only persist, but are increased as contrasting values and performance expectations are imposed by management.[2] The proliferation of audit mechanisms and use of "metrics" to measure merit continues unabated.[3] We see a deterioration of staff student ratios with impact in class size affecting academic workload, as well as professional opportunities.[4] The importance of striving for collaborative relationships with research subjects remains a challenge, as does the problem of how best to respond to events outside the university, particularly the erosion of a robust commitment to access to justice in both the United Kingdom and the United States.[5]

---

[1]The University and College Union (UCU) has recently published a study of contractual practice in university research which confirms this: 'Support for Research Staff' available at: www.ucu.org.uk/media/14251/FOI-2023---support-for-research-staff/pdf/UCU_HE_FOIs_-_research_staff_support_Dec_23.pdf, accessed on 1 February 2024. In the United States, the American Association of University Professors reports that 70% of academic positions are now outside of the tenure track. Data Snapshot: Tenure and Contingency in US Higher Education | AAUP, bit.ly/3Uzxzui

[2]For a recent study see: Lydia Bleasdale, 'Examining Teaching-Focussed Law Teachers Through the Prism of Self-determination Theory' in Caroline Strevens and Emma Jones (eds), *Wellbeing and the Legal Academy* (Springer 2023), pp. 39–55.

[3]For a critical perspective seeking to impose standards see: Academic Analytics Data in the Context of Promotion and Tenure, bit.ly/3UtSCOA

[4]Some things have got better in the United Kingdom, most noteworthy being the successful defence of the Universities Superannuation Scheme (a pension scheme many academics depend upon) by determined action by the UCU over several years of industrial action and negotiation. "UCU wins five year long USS pension dispute" 20 October 2023, available at: https://www.ucu.org.uk/article/13247/UCU-wins-five-year-long-USS-pension-dispute#:~:text=Over%2099%25%20of%20the%2019k,by%20Monday%201%20April%202024, accessed on 27 January 2024.

[5]Recent empirical accounts of the decline approaching collapse of legally aided practitioners in the United Kingdom include: Robyn Lee, Tom Birch and Matthew Humphries, 'Survey of civil legal aid providers in England and Wales', Ministry of Justice 2024, available at: https://assets.publishing.service.gov.uk/media/65aa4068ed27ca000d27b28a/civil-legal-aid-providers-survey.pdf, accessed on 1 February 2024; Daniel Rourke, Ed Cripwell, Joseph Summers and Jo Hynes, "Access to immigration legal aid in 2023: An ocean of unmet need", Public Law Project 2024, available at: https://publiclawproject.org.uk/content/uploads/2023/09/Oceans-of-unmet-need-Sep-2023.pdf, accessed on 1 February

In keeping with the original pieces in *The Law Teacher*, our discussion here is framed in terms of vulnerability theory.[6] Vulnerability theory emphasises the ways in which an institutional focus can illuminate how the political (or "public") shapes and defines the personal (or "private"). In vulnerability theory, the institutional is defined in broad terms,[7] which includes institutional organisation at the macro level – such as the family, market, and state,[8] as well as both the meso level – such as private property, and the corporate form, and micro level – with entities such as the university, local government authorities, and labour unions.[9] The key point for vulnerability theory is that institutions in their various forms structure the interlocking social arrangements in which individuals inevitably find themselves, arrangements that not only provide, but often confine the contexts and the possibilities for action and reaction.[10] In this way,

---

2024; Jon Robins and Daniel Newman, *Justice in a Time of Austerity: Stories from a System in Crisis* (Bristol University Press 2021); James Thornton, *Criminal Justice in Austerity: Legal Aid, Prosecution and the Future of Criminal Legal Practice* (Hart Publishing 2023).

[6] The Vulnerability and Human Condition Initiative (VHC) at Emory Law School began in 2008. It developed from research in the field of feminist jurisprudence and social justice theory. The Feminism and Legal Theory Project (FLT) was begun in 1984 at the University of Wisconsin. Over the past 40 years as it has moved (with Professor Fineman) from Wisconsin to Columbia and then to Cornell and Emory Universities, it has organised a series of workshops, many of which led to publications in journals or as books. An important and unique archive of the work of FLT and VHC (including video recordings of workshops and lectures by visiting scholars) can be found at Emory University School of Law in the Hugh F. MacMillan Law Library, and can be accessed digitally by contacting the archivist. See also the "Women and the Law" collection on HeinOnline. Vulnerability theory operates as a cluster of intellectually linked research endeavours, concentrated in legal scholarship but extending beyond that discipline, as the two chapters (Chapters 6 and 7) in this book by scholars from a medical background illustrate.

[7] Douglass C North, *Institutions, Institutional Change and Economic Performance* (Cambridge University Press 1990) differentiated institutions (macro and meso-institutions) and organisations (micro-institutions) respectively although he accepted that the classification is analytic and can change as the analytical focus changes. Thus, the UK Land Registry is an organisation from the perspective of those who run it and work in it but an institution from the perspective of those who are engaged in transactions with registered land. We could designate these types of institutions by different names as North did, but doing so does not avoid the risk of confusion as the names would shift as the analysis shifted.

[8] Martha Albertson Fineman, *The Autonomy Myth: A Theory of Dependency* (The New Press 2004) identifies these three macro-institutions as fundamental to any adequate account of modern society.

[9] It is often such micro-institutions/organisations that people intend to designate by the term "institution" by which they might refer to the electoral college in the United States, private or public banks, or stock exchanges.

[10] The importance of taking an institutional approach to understanding modern life has been identified many times in different disciplines, the failure to do so generates the "fundamental attribution error" in social psychology: "Our exploration of the intuitive psychologist's shortcomings must start with his general tendency to overestimate the importance of personal or dispositional factors relative to environmental influences", Lee Ross, "The Intuitive Psychologist and His Shortcomings: Distortions in the Attribution Process" p. 173, at p. 184 in Leonard Berkowitz (ed) *Advances in Experimental Social Psychology Vol 10* (Academic Press 1977). In public health, the approach is known as a population approach: Alfredo Morabia, *Population Thinking from the Black Death to COVID-19* (Johns Hopkins University Press 2023). In economics it is associated with the New Institutional Economics approach as well as with economists interested in empirical economics, for example: Anne Case and Angus Deaton, *Deaths of Despair and the Future of Capitalism* (Princeton University Press 2021). It is of course foundational to sociology as illustrated by the classic study: Emile Durkheim, *On Suicide* (Penguin 2006).

the theory concludes that we are all inextricably embedded in social institutions and relationships throughout our lives and in all our various endeavours.[11]

Placing the individual within institutional and relational contexts directs our analytical attention away from narratives that tend to exclusively focus on individual characteristics, failings, abilities, and responsibility to more institutional and structural components. An example of this approach is found in Chapter 2.[12] The analysis in that chapter locates the problems experienced by an individual in the academic workplace within an institutional context, specifically addressing the Law School and University as they have responded to alterations in political order.[13] Thus neo-liberalism in responding to a perceived need to control professional practice, introduced audit mechanisms such as the Research Excellence Framework in the United Kingdom, which sought to hold academics accountable for their outputs. At the same time, under the rubric of New Public Management, managers asserted authority over how academics should perform their tasks using techniques of performance management. These developments have been experienced by academics as increasing their workloads, diminishing their professional autonomy, and forcing them to give unwarranted priority to peripheral activity and are widely denigrated as taking "a tick box approach to the job". Vulnerability theory generalises and problematises such institutional changes by placing the subjective experience of individual academics within these altered institutional structures.

In many ways, vulnerability theory thus represents a "flipping" of the feminist practice which arose from consciousness raising of identifying the personal with the political. By contrast, vulnerability theory looks at how the political (as expressed in institutional arrangements) impacts the personal (or the day-to-day contexts of people's lives).[14] This perspective allows us to see why it is imperative that we address not only individual harm, but also institutional injustice. Unjust institutions tend to impact the lives of all who are bound to interact within them. At the same time a vulnerability approach avoids the tendency of an identity-based perspective centred on discrimination (and perpetrators or victims) to view specific individual actions as the fundamental problem.

---

[11] Martha Albertson Fineman, "Vulnerability and Inevitable Inequality" (2017) 4 *Oslo Law Review* pp. 133, 134: "In considering human vulnerability it is significant that, as embodied beings, individual humans find themselves dependent upon, and embedded within, social relationships and institutions throughout the life-course."

[12] The deployment of the HSE management standards in this chapter is reproduced in a review of empirical studies framed through well-being theory in Caroline Strevens, Rachael Field, and Colin James, "An Analysis of Studies on the Wellbeing of Law Teachers in the UK and Australia in 2020 Using the Lens of Seven Psychosocial Hazards of Academic Work" in Caroline Strevens and Emma Jones (eds), *Wellbeing and the Legal Academy* (Springer 2023), pp. 21–38.

[13] Gary Gerstle, *The Rise and Fall of the Neoliberal Order: America and the World in the Free Market* (Oxford University Press 2022).

[14] Carol Hanisch, "The Personal Is Political" available at: www.carolhanisch.org/CHwritings/PIP.html, accessed on 25 January 2024. For discussion of the origins and contested meanings of the phrase see: Renee Heberle, "The Personal Is Political" in Lisa Disch and Mary Hawkesworth (eds), *The Oxford Handbook of Feminist Theory* (Oxford University Press 2016), p. 593.

All of the chapters in this book employ insights from vulnerability theory to look beyond the individual situation and find the shared experiences and institutional limitations that operate across disparate situations. If so-called neo-liberal discourse is relentlessly individualistic in its orientation, vulnerability theory is equally insistent upon the need to appreciate our common or universal vulnerability and the dependency on institutional structures that it inevitably entails.

One area of mounting concern since the publication of the journal has been threats to the institutional independence of universities and research organisations in the United States and the United Kingdom. As Risa L. Lieberwitz argues, the conduct of university governance is a vital component of academic freedom. In her chapter "Vulnerability theory and higher education" she discusses "faculty academic freedom, job security, and self-governance" which are aspects of institutional or university independence.[15]

University independence as a part of academic freedom has been explicitly recognised by the Council of Europe:[16]

> "Academic freedom should guarantee the right of both institutions and individuals to be protected against public authorities or others."

This statement recognises that university independence is something that needs to be built and does not assume it is an *a priori* given. It must not only be built initially, but also protected as universities as contrived social institutions are vulnerable to encroachments upon their independence from political and market forces.

European and international approaches diverge from the Anglo-American discourse in some interesting ways in the area of academic freedom. Anglo-American discussions tend towards an individual (person or institution) rights perspective. This is clearly illustrated in the narrow focus of this summary of the potential claimants of academic freedom:[17]

> "There has been no agreement on who the beneficiaries of academic freedom are. Professors of course, but what about students and university administrators: are they also legatees of academic freedom?"

While various institutional actors are mentioned, there is no recognition of the claims of the "public" (or society more broadly). Nor is there an appeal based on positioning academic freedom as being a requisite in the abstract search for truth.

A broader approach is suggested by Lyer, Saliba, and Spannagel, who position academic freedom as giving effect to the human right to science:[18]

---

[15]The following discussion was greatly benefited by the paper delivered by Risa L. Liberwitz, "The Critical Role of Faculty Governance to Fulfil the Public Mission of Higher education" at the workshop "Feminist Approaches to State and governance", Emory University School of Law, December 15–16 2023, and the subsequent discussion.

[16]Council of Europe, 2012, para 5, cited by Kirsten Roberts Lyer, Ilyas Saliba, and Janika Spannagel, *University Autonomy Decline: Causes, Responses, and Implications for Academic Freedom* (Routledge 2022), p. 19.

[17]Daniel Gordon, *What is Academic Freedom?: A Century of Debate, 1915–Present* (Routledge 2022), p. 1.

[18]Kirsten Roberts Lyer, Ilyas Saliba, and Janika Spannagel, *University Autonomy Decline: Causes, Responses, and Implications for Academic Freedom* (Routledge 2022), p. 18.

> "Understanding academic freedom in the context of the human right to science, can set clearer parameters for autonomy, understanding that a decline in institutional autonomy in favour of state control is a restriction on the freedom of science that impacts all of society. Framing academic freedom within the right to science, helps to come closer to an understanding of academic freedom (and universities) as key foundations for the search for truth. This approach also shifts academic freedom's focus from being an individual right (e.g., the right to express oneself) to a societal right, and sets it within the expectation that this unrestricted search for truth will ultimately benefit society as a whole."

This approach accords with the insight provided by vulnerability theory: not only people but institutions and endeavours are vulnerable. We should be looking beyond the private interests in considering the value of academic freedom, understanding it as essential from a broader perspective. Employing vulnerability theory opens up the consideration of encroachments on academic freedom in a way that enables us to not only ask whose rights are in issue, but what societal interests are threatened.

With this broader perspective in mind, we also note events in the United States since the publication of the journal that represent an intensification of attacks on academic freedom. There have been two specific and explicit assaults on institutional independence originating from outside the university – political challenges in the form of judicial and legislative actions and threats, and individual donor challenges in the form of withdrawal of funding and support. The pressure on leaders of universities has led to the resignations of the presidents of the University of Pennsylvania and Harvard University.[19] These and related challenges to the independence of universities[20] are too complex and nuanced for us to explore here. Suffice it to say that

[19]"Congressional Committee on Education and the Workforce" hearing "Holding Campus leaders Accountable and Confronting Antisemitism", available at: https://edworkforce.house.gov/calendar/eventsingle.aspx?EventID=409777, accessed on 2 February 2024. Representative Virginia Foxx "Opening Statement", available at: https://edworkforce.house.gov/uploadedfiles/12.5.23_chair_foxx_opening_statement.pdf, accessed on 2 February 2024. Reported by Moustafa Bayoumi, "The Harvard and UPenn presidents walked into a trap in Congress", *The Guardian*, Monday 11 December 2023. Available at: www.theguardian.com/commentisfree/2023/dec/11/the-harvard-and-upenn-presidents-walked-into-a-trap-in-congress, accessed on 2 February 2024, and Josh Moody, "Penn President Resigns After Missteps on Antisemitism" Inside Higher Education, 11 December 2023, available at: www.insidehighered.com/news/governance/executive-leadership/2023/12/11/missteps-antisemitism-prompt-penns-president-resign, accessed on 2 February 2024. Josh Moody, "What Do Universities Owe Their Donors?: Inside Higher Education, 2 November 2023. Available at: www.insidehighered.com/news/governance/executive-leadership/2023/11/02/what-do-universities-owe-their-donors, accessed on 2 February 2024.

[20]Some of the attacks have been on policies to ensure Diversity, Equity, and Inclusion (DEI), which followed the decisions in *Students for Fair Admissions v. Harvard* (*SFA v Harvard*) and *Students for Fair Admissions v. University of North Carolina*: *Students for Fair Admissions v. Harvard* and *Students for Fair Admissions v. University of North Carolina* 600 U.S. 181 (2023). Amanda Heidt, "Universities axe diversity statements in wake of US Supreme Court ruling on affirmative action" 27 September 2023 *Nature*. Jack Stripling, "DeSantis signs bill to defund DEI programs at Florida's public colleges", 15 May 2023, *Washington Post*. Available at: www.washingtonpost.com/education/2023/05/15/desantis-defunds-dei-programs-florida-colleges/, accessed on 2 February 2024.

attacks on institutional independence led almost immediately to attacks on academic freedom in the classroom.[21]

Recent challenges to academic freedom in the United Kingdom also have been serious. There are two areas of concern. Firstly, intrusion on the independence and integrity of the public research funding body – United Kingdom Research and Innovation (UKRI) by Michelle Donelan.[22] Secondly, the creation of files and records by governmental departments that were used to deny public platforms to academics who have been critical of the administration.[23] Michelle Donelan's use of public communications to criticise individuals and the expert advice they provided to the UKRI led to a successful legal challenge against the minister.[24] The revelation of the practice by government departments of keeping files on academics, and based on the contents of these files, and of supressing contributions by academics to government-supported events, led to the launch of a campaign by the UCU and successful challenges in individual cases.[25]

As stated earlier, vulnerability theory applies not only to analysis of the position of individuals, but extends to the social and political institutions in which all individuals are inevitably located. Ironically, masking the attacks on academic freedom by both the United States and the United Kingdom governments is a rhetoric of protection for

---

[21]"What the Florida DEI Bill Means to Us", 24 May 2023, The King Centre, available at https://thekingcenter.org/what-the-florida-dei-bill-means-to-us/, accessed on 2 February 2024. Florida Department of Education 17 January 2024, "State Board of Education Passes Rule to Permanently Prohibit DEI in the Florida College System", available at: www.fldoe.org/newsroom/latest-news/state-board-of-education-passes-rule-to-permanently-prohibit-dei-in-the-florida-college-system.stml, accessed on 2 February 2024.

[22]Michelle Donelan to Dame Ottoline Leyser: https://twitter.com/michelledonelan/status/1718291791861182514/photo/1, accessed on 20 February 2024. Letter from UCU to Dame Ottoline Leyser: www.ucu.org.uk/media/14178/UKRI-Letter/pdf/UKRILetter.pdf, accessed on 27 January 2024. https://exposedcampaign.org.uk/, accessed on 20 February 2024. UKRI, Response to the open letter from the Secretary of State at: www.ukri.org/news/response-to-the-open-letter-from-the-secretary-of-state/, accessed on 27 January 2024.

[23]Anna Fazackerley, "Revealed: UK government keeping files on education critics' social media activity", *Observer*, 30 September, www.theguardian.com/education/2023/sep/30/revealed-uk-government-keeping-files-on-education-critics-social-media-activity. Anna Fazackerley, "UK government keeping files on teaching assistants' and librarians' internet activity", *Observer*, 21 October 2023 available at: www.theguardian.com/politics/2023/oct/21/uk-government-keeping-files-on-teaching-assistants-and-librarians-internet-activity. Anna Fazackerley, "'Shocking' scale of UK government's secret files on critics revealed", *The Observer*, 18 Nov 2023, available at: www.theguardian.com/politics/2023/nov/18/shocking-scale-of-uk-governments-secret-files-on-critics-revealed. All accessed on 27 January 2024.

[24]Chas Geiger, "Michelle Donelan's false Hamas claim about academic cost taxpayer £15,000", *BBC News*, 6 March 2024, available at: www.bbc.co.uk/news/uk-politics-68496320, accessed on 19 March 2024.

[25]"Exposed: UCU's campaign to uncover government interference, monitoring and meddling in our sector", available at: https://exposedcampaign.org.uk/, accessed on 19 March 2024. Anna Fazackerley, "Revealed: UK government keeping files on education critics' social media activity" *Observer*, 30 September, www.theguardian.com/education/2023/sep/30/revealed-uk-government-keeping-files-on-education-critics-social-media-activity, accessed on 19 March 2024.

freedom of speech and enhancement of equality, even as the attacks undermine those very principles. Such "doublespeak" undermines and impoverishes public discourse.[26]

If academic freedom and integrity are essential in the generation and dissemination of knowledge and education is key to the development of an informed, effective, and just society, then obstructing academic functioning for politically partisan reasons undermines the public good. In the words of Aaron Bradbury, a principal lecturer at Nottingham Trent University, when there were threats to cancel the conference at which he had been invited to speak:[27]

> "To be told that we couldn't have this debate felt like we were living in a dictatorship, not a democracy... We were due to talk about nurturing and early child development. It wasn't some covert stuff about infiltrating Russia."

A main area of threat to academic freedom in both the United Kingdom and the United States since the special edition of *The Law Teacher* was published has been on policies implementing principles of diversity and inclusion. While these have been of concern to the academy (and society) for decades, recent attention seems to have triggered a highly politicised and destructive attack in the form of judicial and legislative changes in the United States and overreach by the executive in the United Kingdom. All aspects of academic freedom have been under pressure, but the freedom to teach, freedom of academics to comment in non-academic fora, and the institutional independence of universities have been under most pressure. Institutional independence, and academic freedoms more generally, are vulnerable, and building resilience remains a central concern for all those concerned with the public right to truth.

As the articles included in this book make clear attacks upon academic freedom are experienced as attacks upon academics. The internalisation of the ethics of an academic discipline give existential resilience to academics, and attacks: upon the pursuit of truth in research, upon attempts to support students and academics from groups who have been and are subject to discrimination, upon academic engagement with public fora in order to disseminate their research and serve the public; reduce both personal resilience and the public interest in academia as a source of science and truth.

---

[26]The word "doublespeak" was coined by George Orwell for use in his novel *1984.* Whilst systemic attempts to supress critical academic speech were underway the legislature was passing the Higher Education (Freedom of Speech) Act 2023.

[27]Anna Fazackerley, "Revealed: UK government keeping files on education critics' social media activity" *Observer*, 30 September, www.theguardian.com/education/2023/sep/30/revealed-uk-government-keeping-files-on-education-critics-social-media-activity

Introduction

Graham Ferris and Martha Albertson Fineman

This special issue is made up of articles developed from papers first delivered at an international workshop on vulnerability and academic labour in Nottingham, an event supported by *The Law Teacher*, the Vulnerability and the Human Condition Initiative (VHCI), and Nottingham Trent University. The initial impetus was very specific and personal – a realisation amongst members of *The Law Teacher* editorial board that our after business conversation was dominated by concerns around the relentless demands being made on ourselves and our colleagues by our roles as legal educators. It was clear that wellbeing concerns went beyond the student body and encompassed the academic workforce, and the situation felt new and threatening.

Graham Ferris, serving multiple roles – staff member at Nottingham Trent, member of *The Law Teacher* board, and visiting scholar at Emory University – approached the parties who sponsored the workshop and took his place in the organising committee with Professors Martha Albertson Fineman and Stu Marvel from Emory. The workshop was successful and identified enough quality work to support a special issue and here we are.

In the face of a global pandemic it is clear that the vulnerability of both people and institutions cannot be denied. Modernity may have freed those in the developed world from some risks (such as famine), but it has generated its own set of risks (such as the unprecedently swift spreading of global pandemics). Vulnerability theory is based on the realisation that vulnerability is a central and inescapable aspect of the human condition, arising from our embodiment and mandating our continuous dependence on social institutions and relationships. The articles in this special issue all draw upon vulnerability theory to try and understand what its implications are for legal education, legal educators, academics, and our societies today.

Legal education and legal educators face inherent internal tensions across time and place. One might give as examples such narrow concerns as divergences in staff and student expectations around the relationship between legal education and preparation for practice, or the problems posed to legal education by any attempt to prepare students for the pressures of the workplace upon ethical conduct. This special issue is primarily concerned not with these internal pressures but with external social, economic and political pressures that have an impact upon the conduct of legal education in the modern world. These external or broad pressures operate at an international and systemic level, although they are mediated through more local institutions.

This special issue examines the vulnerability of professional education to social, economic, and political pressures across three jurisdictions (England and Wales, the USA, and Brazil). These pressures threaten both the integrity of professional education and the wellbeing of those who work within it, although there is resistance to these pressures in defence of a principled education. Our focus is unusually broad because these pressures do not originate in, nor are they confined to, legal education. Because those pressures are truly systemic, they require an organising analytical framework capable of working at the level of generality appropriate to systemic phenomena.

The papers explore a range of issues: modern developments in the management of universities, the consequences of audit models of control of academic work, the problems posed for legal educators by the erosion of areas of practice, the vexed question of what effects academics should seek to have outside academia, professional ethics, and the ethics of research and community engagement. In all these areas there are threats to resilience, but also resistance to these threats.

The resilience of legal education is not merely a matter for those concerned with legal education. Legal education can either enhance social resilience or undermine it. Thus, the papers consider not only the resilience of academics, law schools, and universities, but the effects on the social public goods that legal education and other professional education may provide or enhance.

We open this special issue with an account of the struggle for a higher education focused on the US and UK educational systems. Risa L. Lieberwitz in "Vulnerability Theory and Higher Education" argues that universities are organisations in which control, ownership, and purpose are disputed. Despite this struggle, she argues academic staff necessarily lie at the centre of the university, regardless of contemporary corporatist or managerial pretensions. She shows how the social roles and educational missions of universities require this staff centrality, and how academics have collectively organised and fought for recognition of their legitimate claims of place.

We begin with the university because legal education is predominantly based there. Even where it is not so based, the university sector dominates perceptions and remains the model for the delivery of legal and professional education generally. The university is the most important mediating organisation between broader pressures and working academics. Therefore, it is at this level that any effective amelioration of academic labour must start. That shared interest with other academics necessitates legal academics turning towards non-legal academics in making a common case for the public good contributions of university education and research.

Lieberwitz uses vulnerability theory to examine the university, the society it serves, and its workforce. Just as every individual is vulnerable, so are human institutions such as the university. The university as an organisational form has been tremendously resilient. However, as Lieberwitz shows recent developments risk eroding this resilience and undermining the implicit *modus operandi* between academics, universities, and society through erosion of shared purpose in advancing the public good and the substitution of a collection of individual and disparate interests in an unstable concatenation.

Graham Ferris, in "Undermining Resilience: How the Modern UK University Manufactures Heightened Vulnerability in Legal Academics and What Is to Be Done", situates the law school in an even broader context, that of the regulatory state of the neoliberal age. He uses vulnerability theory to highlight the problems the modern political environment generates and suggest how academics can resist. Although focused on the UK, the analysis of how neoliberalism has an impact upon the resilience of academics is of wider relevance. He argues we must lose the ultra-individualistic focus of neoliberal analysis and look to the institutional factors that support or degrade resilience. The article integrates vulnerability theory with a health and safety conceptual framework in order to facilitate local resistance by academics to systemic problems.

In "Rethinking the Neo-liberal University: Embracing Vulnerability in English Law Schools?" Doug Morrison and Jessica Guth bring the analysis closer to home, focusing on the neoliberal law school in England and Wales. They also highlight the potential for vulnerability theory to illuminate the problems of the modern law school. However, the article argues the theory operates at too high a level of generality to inform resistance to these problems at the level of the individual law school. Thus, the authors suggest there remains a need to search for another theoretical framework to support effective resistance and protection of the wellbeing of individual academics.

Continuing with a focus on the UK Nicola Harris, Roxanna Dehaghari and Daniel Newman examine the ethical and practical problems of a legal education that supports a collapsing area of practice in "Vulnerability, the Future of the Criminal Defence Profession, and the Implications for Teaching and Learning". Vulnerability theory clearly states that institutions and practices are vulnerable, not just individuals, and the work of criminal defence in England and Wales is a practice area that is under existential threat. The authors show how this educational problem is addressed at Cardiff, and how this in turn permits the academy to support an area of practice vital for society and the rule of law.

The role of legal education in addressing social problems is an issue further developed by Fabrizia Serafim in "Vulnerability Theory as a Tool Against a Banking Model of Legal Education". She introduces a Brazilian educational practice of "extensão", thereby broadening our focus in two dimensions: to encompass non-UK and US legal education and suggesting a potentially more democratic and progressive Brazilian version of "impact" in academia.

The constitutionally embedded concept of extensão calls for academics to devote some time and resources to work that has beneficial effects beyond the academy. The concept has become contested, but Serafim argues it can and should be understood and enacted through practices that accord with educational principles identified by the Brazilian educational theorist Paulo Freire. She argues a vulnerability theory lens enables the analyst to identify the crucial pedagogical issues raised by debates around the meaning of extensão and the purpose of higher education. She contends specifically that it permits the legal educator to address a lacuna in the work of Freire, who focused upon the education of ordinary people, rather than elites such as lawyers.

Of course, it is not only activities demarcated as impact in the UK, or extensão in Brazil, that have effects upon people beyond academia. Nor is it only in their teaching role that academics need to be aware of the perspectives of those outside the academic circle. In "The Positive and Negative Roles of Grant Funding as Mechanisms for Societal Transformation and the Development of Community Resilience", Joan Wilson and WR Sexson broaden the focus again to take in another type of professional education, specifically medicine, and shift the attention from academic teaching to academic research.

The impact of academic research upon communities who are the subjects for that research should be of immediate concern to any researcher whose work involves investigation of people's lived experience. Wilson and Sexson concentrate on poor neighbourhood communities in Atlanta, Georgia, but the principles apply far more generally as consistent with vulnerability theory it is not only the poor who are vulnerable. They argue that the perspective of the community under investigation is vital to research, both because the impact of the research on the community is an ethically vital aspect of the research and because a failure to draw the community in and respond to its needs and concerns leads to a collapse in the relationship between researcher and researched, resulting in the failure of the research in the short or long term.

The final article is immediately concerned with medical education in the USA. In "The University's Fragile Role in Fostering Societal Resilience by Facilitating the Development of Community-Engaged Professionalism", WR Sexson and MJoan Wilson engage with an issue that is also familiar in legal education – the instruction and purpose of professional ethics in professional education. In the spirit of treating professionalism seriously, the article reviews the origins of professional ethics and describes a teaching programme in Atlanta that incorporates insights from vulnerability theory into its teaching of ethics.

As with the preceding three articles, this final article is concerned with the effects of professional education beyond the academy. Whilst professional ethics can serve to support the resilience of the individual practitioner through its role as an existential asset for resilience, Sexson and Wilson focus upon the potential benefits beyond academia of a broad commitment to justice embedded in medical ethics. Obviously, this potential finds a parallel in legal ethics. As illustrated by the educational practice of Harris, Dehaghani and Newman, legal education can and should take an interest in the future social roles and performance of its alumni. As vulnerable legal academics serve as a source of resilience for their students and society, they also can provide a bulwark against depredations imposed by neoliberal dogma.

As initially argued by Lieberwitz, there is a need to claim and strengthen the salience of older understanding of academic, professional, and legal values in the modern law school, as well as in the broader university and public sphere. When we attend to our own vulnerability, we are better able to understand and respond to the needs and expectations of others. From the perspective provided by vulnerability theory we can transcend analyses that see vulnerability as an individual failing and focus instead on the pressing contemporary need for institutional norms and practices that support resilience.

Vulnerability theory and higher education

Risa L. Lieberwitz

ABSTRACT

Vulnerability theory stresses the role of an active state that is responsive to our common human needs: health, safety, sustenance, shelter, education, and fulfilling work. This article studies institutions of higher education in the US and UK through the lens of vulnerability theory, examining the role of the state to serve the public interest through its colleges and universities. The history of higher education in the US and UK, particularly in the 1950s and 1960s, reveals advances in the development of institutions with a public mission committed to broad student access, strong faculty employment rights, and the public domain of research and knowledge. Since the 1980s, however, the imposition of state neoliberal policy has undermined the public mission of higher education through cuts in public funding, rising tuition and student debt, contingent faculty employment, and commercialization of academic research. Such changes have weakened the institutional structure of higher education, leaving universities ill-equipped to resist the most recent political and ideological attacks on intellectuals and progressive social movements that are nurtured in higher education institutions. At the same time, organising by faculty and student unions and professional organisations presents the potential for collective action as a form of resilience, resistance, and social change

This article studies institutions of higher education in the US and UK through the lens of vulnerability theory. Part I of the article examines the role of the state to serve the public interest through its colleges and universities.[1] In the current neoliberal era, it may be difficult to imagine a society where the state is responsive to human needs, including state support for higher education as a public good. Yet the history of higher education in the US and UK, particularly in the 1950s and 1960s, reveals advances in the development of institutions with a public mission committed to broad student access, strong faculty employment rights, and the public domain of research and knowledge.

Part II analyses the imposition of state neoliberal policy on vulnerable institutions of higher education since the 1980s, characterised by cuts in public funding, rising tuition and student debt, contingent faculty employment, and commercialisation of academic research. By commodifying teaching and research and expanding the ranks of contingent faculty, these institutional changes have undermined the essential elements of universities' ability to serve the public interest. As discussed in Part III, such changes have weakened the

[1]This article will use the term "university" to refer, generally, to colleges and universities.

institutional structure of higher education, leaving universities ill-equipped to resist the most recent political and ideological attacks on intellectuals and progressive social movements that are nurtured in higher education institutions. At the same time, organising by faculty and student unions and professional organisations presents the potential for collective action as a form of resilience, resistance, and social change.

I. Higher education in the public interest

A. Overview of vulnerability theory and higher education

While the US and UK do not treat post-secondary education as a universal right, on a policy level there is broad agreement that "[i]nstitutions of higher education are conducted for the common good and not to further the interest of either the individual teacher or the institution as a whole. The common good depends upon the free search for truth and its free exposition."[2] Vulnerability theory is helpful in understanding the complexity inherent in creating higher education institutions that achieve this goal. Consistent with vulnerability theory, defining higher education institutions as having a public mission recognises their societal role in responding to human needs and contributing to the public welfare.[3] Colleges and universities carry out this mission through multiple functions: teaching that develops students' interests and abilities; research that contributes to the public domain of ideas and knowledge; and public engagement that contributes to debate and policy-making about social, economic, or political issues. The state has an essential role in creating and shaping higher education institutions that can fulfil these social functions. This is not a simple matter, requiring that states fund higher education institutions, while also respecting university autonomy and faculty academic freedom. The state must also protect universities' independence from conflicting interests of third parties, including donors and industry. At the same time, the state should protect the academic freedom of faculty and students from interference by the university administration.

State resources take various forms, including full funding of a public universities, public funding to both public and private universities, tax-exempt status, and public policy protecting universities' institutional independence from governmental interference. Further, the state can support faculty and students through law and public policy protecting individual faculty employment rights of academic freedom, job security, and due process, collective faculty rights to unionise, and student rights to organise. In the terms of vulnerability theory, these state resources and legal protections provide the foundation for strong and resilient higher education institutions that serve the public interest, while not pressuring universities to please the public. As Berdahl explains, "Universities have generally had ambivalent relations with their surrounding societies:

---

[2]American Association of University Professors, "1940 Statement of Principles on Academic Freedom and Tenure" in *Policy Documents and Reports* (11th edn, Johns Hopkins University Press 2015) 14. See also, in the UK, the Robbins Report: "[E]ducation ministers intimately to ultimate ends, in developing man's capacity to understand, to contemplate and to create. And it is a characteristic of the aspirations of this age to feel that, where there is capacity to pursue such activities, there that capacity should be fostered. The good society desires equality of opportunity for its citizens to become not merely good producers but also good men and women." Committee on Higher Education, *Higher Education: Report of the Committee Appointed by the Prime Minister under the Chairmanship of Lord Robbins, 1961–63* (Cmnd 2154, 1963) (hereinafter, Robbins Report) para 33 <www.educationengland.org.uk/documents/robbins/robbins1963.html>.

[3]On vulnerability theory, see, eg Martha Albertson Fineman, "The Vulnerable Subject and the Responsive State" (2010) 60 Emory LJ 251; Martha Albertson Fineman, "The Vulnerable Subject: Anchoring Equality in the Human Condition" (2008) 20 Yale JL & Feminism 1.

both involved and withdrawn; both serving and criticising; both needing and being needed."[4]

This description of higher education in the public interest resonates with elements that are present in the US and UK systems. International comparisons should always recognise the significance of historical, social, and cultural differences. Certainly, in comparing the US and UK systems of higher education, a major structural difference exists between the UK national system as contrasted with the decentralised system of public and private universities in the US. However, significant parallels do appear in the evolution of the modern university in the US and UK and the expansion and contraction of a public interest model of higher education.

B. The public mission of higher education in the US and UK

In the post-World War II period, particularly in the 1950s and 1960s, state support for higher education in the US and UK helped create the conditions for universities with a public mission. Public funding increased, leading to a growth in the number and size of universities, which broadened student access and created the need for more faculty, whose conditions of employment included academic freedom and promotion review on a tenure-track system. The road to this expansion point was uneven. Given their different histories and social conditions, the US and UK did not follow the same timeline and events. However, highlighting developments during the twentieth century provides insight into common aspects of both countries' progression towards a public interest model of higher education.

1. Higher education as a public good

The modern university in the US and UK came out of an ecclesiastical tradition of elite institutions of higher education, open only to young men from the economically or politically powerful classes.[5] Yet the period of the late nineteenth and early twentieth centuries was also one of great social turmoil with the development of capitalism during the era of industrialisation, as well as major advances in scientific methods and knowledge. The modern university evolved into a secular institution with an expanded curriculum that encompassed the humanities, natural sciences, and the growing social sciences. Faculty disciplinary expertise in the expanding curriculum created the conditions for their independence from university governing boards made up of clergy or businessmen.

In the US, these conditions led to the formation of the American Association of University Professors (AAUP), whose 1915 Declaration of Principles describes the mission of higher education and the role of faculty to serve the public interest rather than private proprietary interests.[6] These principles established that for universities to act as a "public trust", faculty must exercise academic freedom to teach, research, and engage

[4]Robert Berdahl, "Academic Freedom, Autonomy and Accountability in British Universities" (1990) 15 Studies in Higher Education 169, 170 .

[5]See Richard Hofstadter and Walter P Metzger, *The Development of Academic Freedom in the United States* (Columbia University Press 1955) 61–78, 365–66; Bernard Longden and Charles Bélanger, "Universities: Public Good or Private Profit" (2013) 35 Journal of Higher Education Policy and Management 501, 510.

[6]American Association of University Professors, "1915 Declaration of Principles in Academic Freedom and Tenure" in *Policy Documents and Reports* (11th edn, Johns Hopkins University Press 2015) 3 (hereinafter, 1915 Declaration).

in public speech, without interference from university governing boards or administrators who may have conflicting private or political interests.[7] To preserve their independence, faculty must have strong job security of tenure and engage in collective self-governance over academic matters, including peer evaluation for hiring and promotion.

It was not until the post-World War II period in the US that public funding was provided at levels that supported broad national growth in universities and significantly expanded student access to higher education. The federal GI Bill created opportunities for returning members of the armed forces to attend universities, although the benefits went primarily to white men.[8] States expanded the number and size of two-year and four-year public universities, in what has been called the "massification" of higher education from 1960 through the mid-1970s, with state and federal funding being used to maintain low tuition levels.[9]

In the UK, the commitment to publicly supported higher education was slower in coming, given the entrenched class-based hierarchy of universities such as Oxford and Cambridge.[10] However, when the UK made the commitment to public higher education, the changes were arguably broader and deeper than in the US. Two waves of significant expansion of public higher education have been identified.[11] The first was in the 1960s, before and after the government-commissioned Robbins Report recommended, in 1963, that the existing higher education institutions should be viewed as a system, to be expanded with publicly funded institutions to meet the public's interest in and need for higher education.[12] As Holmwood and Bhambra note, this expansion "[i]n effect … would render private schools anomalous".[13] During the 1960s, the number of publicly funded universities increased significantly, including the civic universities such as Sussex, York, and East Anglia.[14] A second wave of expansion occurred at the end of 1980s and into the early 1990s, with legislation enabling the UK government to grant university status to existing educational institutions, including the former polytechnics.[15]

---

[7]1915 Declaration (n 6) 7.

[8]Dongbin Kim and John L Rury, "The Changing Profile of College Access: The Truman Commission and Enrollment Patterns in the Post-War Era" (2007) 47 History of Education Quarterly 302, 305, 324.

[9]Patricia J Gumport and others, "Trends in United States Higher Education from Massification to Post Massification" (National Center for Postsecondary Improvement, School of Education, Stanford University 1997) 2–12 <https://web.stanford.edu/group/ncpi/cresearchers/organizationalimprovement.html> accessed 10 October 2020; Dongbin Kim and John L Rury, "The Changing Profile of College Access: The Truman Commission and Enrollment Patterns in the Post-War Era" (2007) 47 History of Education Quarterly 302, 302–13.

[10]John Holmwood and Gurminder K Bhambra, "The Attack on Education as a Social Right" (2012) 111 South Atlantic Quarterly 392, 395. Free public secondary school education was provided in England and Wales only with the passage of the Education Act 1944. Holmwood and Bhambra 395.

[11]Ken Mayhew, Cécile Deer and Mehak Dua, "The Move to Mass Higher Education in the UK: Many Questions and Some Answers" (2004) 30 Oxford Review of Education 65, 66.

[12]Robbins Report (n 2) para 18–20; Ken Mayhew, Cécile Deer and Mehak Dua, "The Move to Mass Higher Education in the UK: Many Questions and Some Answers" (2004) 30 Oxford Review of Education 65, 66; John Holmwood and Gurminder K Bhambra, "The Attack on Education as a Social Right" (2012) 111 South Atlantic Quarterly 392, 395–96.

[13]John Holmwood and Gurminder K Bhambra, "The Attack on Education as a Social Right" (2012) 111 South Atlantic Quarterly 392, 396.

[14]Ken Mayhew, Cécile Deer and Mehak Dua, "The Move to Mass Higher Education in the UK: Many Questions and Some Answers" (2004) 30 Oxford Review of Education 65, 66.

[15]Ken Mayhew, Cécile Deer and Mehak Dua, "The Move to Mass Higher Education in the UK: Many Questions and Some Answers" (2004) 30 Oxford Review of Education 65, 66. See Further and Higher Education Act 1992 <www.legislation.gov.uk/ukpga/1992/13/contents> accessed 25 January 2021.

Although this second wave of expansion has been identified as resulting in "a mass higher education system",[16] it was not as well funded as the first wave in the 1960s.[17]

In the "massification" of higher education in both countries, enrolment increased for working class students, women, and students of colour.[18] Opening access to a broader range of students benefits the university, which gains from the ideas, creativity, and experience the students bring to the institution. Further, such class, gender, and racial diversity increases the potential for student organising around social justice issues. In the 1960s, student activists engaged in mass protests addressing the most burning political issues of the times, including social movements for civil rights, Black Power, feminism, and resistance to the Vietnam War.[19] Students integrated their political activism with demands for democratic participation in university policy-making, including curriculum, academic programmes, and transparency and ethical accountability in academic research programmes.

In the post-World War II period in the US, the federal government expanded public funding for academic research, particularly in science and engineering. Since 1960, federal funding has constituted the majority of university research support.[20] In the UK, prior to 1988, public research funding was allocated in block grants by the University Grants Committee and Research Councils, on which academics were the dominant presence.[21]

The state's commitment to public higher education with broad student access builds individual and institutional resilience, which ultimately benefits the democratic goals of the broader society. Students discover their interests and passions, gain knowledge, develop skills of critical thinking, and broaden their personal and professional relationships. Further, the state helps build individual and institutional resilience by supporting teaching and research that questions the status quo, enables faculty to follow new research paths, and creates a venue for students and faculty to organise around ideas

[16]Ken Mayhew, Cécile Deer and Mehak Dua, "The Move to Mass Higher Education in the UK: Many Questions and Some Answers" (2004) 30 Oxford Review of Education 65, 66, citing Peter Scott, *The Meanings of Mass Higher Education* (SRHE/Open University Press 1995).

[17]Ken Mayhew, Cécile Deer and Mehak Dua, "The Move to Mass Higher Education in the UK: Many Questions and Some Answers" (2004) 30 Oxford Review of Education 65, 66.

[18]Patricia J Gumport and others, "Trends in United States Higher Education from Massification to Post Massification" (National Center for Postsecondary Improvement, School of Education, Stanford University 1997) 4–6 <https://web.stanford.edu/group/ncpi/cresearchers/organizationalimprovement.html> accessed 10 October 2020; Dongbin Kim and John L Rury, "The Changing Profile of College Access: The Truman Commission and Enrollment Patterns in the Post-War Era" (2007) 47 History of Education Quarterly 302, 322–25; Ceryn Evans and others, "A Liberal Higher Education for All? The Massification of Higher Education and Its Implications for Graduates' Participation in Civil Society" (2020) Higher Education (forthcoming) <https://doi.org/10.1007/s10734-020-00554-x> accessed 14 October 2020.

[19]Caroline Hoefferle, *British Student Activism in the Long Sixties* (Routledge 2012); Peter Halewood and Donna Young, "Rule of Law, Activism, and Equality: Growing Antisubordination Norms within the Neoliberal University" (2017) 50 John Marshall Law Review 249, 253–55; Dongbin Kim and John L Rury, "The Changing Profile of College Access: The Truman Commission and Enrollment Patterns in the Post-War Era" (2007) 47 History of Education Quarterly 302, 309–10.

[20]American Association for the Advancement of Science, "R&D at Colleges and Universities" (2018) <www.aaas.org/programs/r-d-budget-and-policy/rd-colleges-and-universities> accessed 25 January 2021; Risa L Lieberwitz, "University-Industry Relations in the United States: Serving Private Interests" in James L Turk (ed), *Academic Freedom in Conflict: The Struggle Over Free Speech Rights in the University* (James Lorimer & Company, Ltd 2014) 252.

[21]Robert Berdahl, "Academic Freedom, Autonomy and Accountability in British Universities" (1990) 15 Studies in Higher Education 169; Ken Mayhew, Cécile Deer and Mehak Dua, "The Move to Mass Higher Education in the UK: Many Questions and Some Answers" (2004) 30 Oxford Review of Education 65, 69.

for social change. Such resilience is essential to build a lasting and dynamic system of education, which "make[s] university education widely available beyond a privately educated elite ...".[22] Moreover, providing access to tuition-free or low-tuition universities liberates students to pursue their interests rather than simply a vocation. Mayhew and others stress the non-instrumentalist nature of the 1963 Robbins Report, which advocated that "courses of higher education should be available for all those who are qualified by ability and attainment to pursue them and who wish to do so".[23] While the Robbins Report also included the economic benefits of higher education as rationales for public funding, the broader social vision of education is based on the value of self-actualisation. Holmwood and Bhambra describe the mass expansion of public universities as providing higher education as a social right of citizenship to a public good "designed to facilitate the exercise of [classic] liberal rights" such as freedom of speech and association, suffrage, and private property.[24]

The description of a commitment in the US and UK to higher education in the public interest is not an expression of nostalgia for halcyon days that, in fact, never existed. Higher education as a public good is an ideal that was partially realised with the development of the modern university, commitment to academic freedom, and expanded student access to higher education. These advances laid the institutional foundation upon which to strengthen university policies and practice in the public interest. This potential coexisted with the reality that education has long served as a vehicle for preparing future employees in capitalist enterprises.[25] In this historical and institutional context, defining the public interest has been and remains contested.

2. Faculty academic freedom, job security, and self-governance

For higher education to fulfil a public mission, the labour conditions of faculty must enhance the interrelated professional norms of academic freedom, tenure, and joint/shared governance. Strong job security of tenure protects faculty ability to exercise their academic freedom without pressure, censorship or retaliation by the university administration, government, or donors. Faculty shared governance and academic freedom "are inextricably linked", respecting collective faculty authority over academic matters such as curriculum and peer review, which are foundational to fulfilling the university's public mission.[26] In other areas, including budgetary matters, shared governance entails active consultation between faculty and the university administration.

Prior to the ascendance of neoliberalism in the 1980s, academic freedom, tenure, and shared governance were deeply ingrained in the faculty labour structure in US and UK higher education. In both countries, these norms developed outside the legal system, which has contributed to both their strength and their weakness. Institutional acceptance and individual internalisation of these professional norms treated as "extra-legal" rights create the expectation that university policies, practices, and decision-making will be consistent with foundational academic values. The lack of legal

[22] John Holmwood and Gurminder K Bhambra, "The Attack on Education as a Social Right" (2012) 111 South Atlantic Quarterly 392, 395–96.

[23] Robbins Report (n 2) para 31; Ken Mayhew, Cécile Deer and Mehak Dua, "The Move to Mass Higher Education in the UK: Many Questions and Some Answers" (2004) 30 Oxford Review of Education 65, 68.

[24] John Holmwood and Gurminder K Bhambra, "The Attack on Education as a Social Right" (2012) 111 South Atlantic Quarterly 392, 393.

[25] David Harvie, "Alienation, Class and Enclosure in UK Universities" (2000) 71 Capital and Class 103, 104–05.

[26] American Association of University Professors, "On the Relationship of Faculty Governance to Academic Freedom" in *Policy Documents and Reports* (11th edn, Johns Hopkins University Press 2015) 123, 125.

protection, however, makes the professional norms exposed to erosion by economic and political forces of privatisation.

Academic freedom is not well protected in positive law in either the UK or US. The Education Reform Act 1988 in the UK provides a right of academic freedom only in conjunction with abolishing the tenure system, leaving faculty to raise an unjust dismissal claim only after being discharged.[27] Given the absence of a constitution in the UK, there can be no constitutional right of academic freedom. Despite the US Supreme Court's description of academic freedom as a "special concern" of the First Amendment,[28] private university faculty are not covered by this constitutional protection, which restricts only "state action". Even for public university faculty, First Amendment rights have been severely restricted by Supreme Court decisions narrowing the scope of constitutional rights of public employees.[29]

Even without legal protection, however, academic freedom in both the UK and US has been embedded in higher education institutional norms and policies and the definition of individual academic freedom is similar. As the 1963 Robbins Report stated, "For the individual teacher academic freedom means the absence of discriminatory treatment on grounds of race, sex, religion and politics; and the right to teach according to his own conception of fact and truth, rather than according to any pre-determined orthodoxy. It involves, further, freedom to publish and, subject to the proper performance of allotted duties, freedom to pursue what personal studies or researches are congenial."[30] In the US, the AAUP definition of academic freedom, which has been widely adopted in university policies, protects "freedom of inquiry and research; freedom of teaching within the university or college; and freedom of extramural utterance and action".[31] In both countries, academic freedom has been protected through the job security of tenure and through faculty self-governance. In the US, the AAUP was instrumental in establishing the tenure system, which is notable given the dominance in the US of the common law doctrine of employment-at-will. In the UK, faculty tenure rights were consistent with the broader norm of "just cause" in government policy since the mid-1960s, followed by legislation in 1971.[32] In both countries, universities have recognised faculty self-governance through peer review in hiring and promotions and in faculty collective authority over academic programme and curricular development.

Despite the existence of professional academic norms, administration–faculty relationships are often in tension. Without legislative protection, legal rights enforcement depends on individual employment contracts or collective bargaining agreements. In

---

[27] Terence Karran and Lucy Mallinson, "Academic Freedom in the U.K.: Legal and Normative Protection in a Comparative Context" (Report for the University and College Union, May 2017) 6, 15 (hereinafter "Academic Freedom in the U.K.") <www.ucu.org.uk/article/1865/Site-search?q=karran> accessed 11 October 2020.

[28] *Keyishian v Board of Regents*, 385 US 589, 603 (1967), "Our Nation is deeply committed to safeguarding academic freedom, which is of transcendent value to all of us and not merely to the teachers concerned. That freedom is therefore a special concern of the First Amendment, which does not tolerate laws that cast a pall of orthodoxy over the classroom."

[29] Risa L Lieberwitz, "The Corporatization of the University: Distance Learning at the Cost of Academic Freedom?" (2002) 12 Boston University Public Interest Law Journal 73, 89–90.

[30] Robbins Report (n 2) para 705.

[31] 1915 Declaration (n 6) 4. See also 1940 Statement 14; American Association of University Professors, "Policies on Academic Freedom, Dismissal for Cause, Financial Exigency, and Program Discontinuance" (Report, 2020) <www.aaup.org/report/policies-academic-freedom-dismissal-cause-financial-exigency-and-program-discontinuance> accessed 11 October 2020 (73% of 1170 US four-year colleges studied had academic freedom policies based directly on the AAUP's 1940 Statement).

[32] See Janice R Bellace, "A Right of Fair Dismissal: Enforcing a Statutory Guarantee" (1983) 16 U Mich J L Reform 207, 218–31 <https://repository.law.umich.edu/mjlr/vol16/iss2/4> accessed 14 October 2020

both countries, faculty unionisation took hold in the 1960s. In the UK, over the decades since the 1950s formalisation of faculty unionisation, the national unions have merged into the current University and College Union (UCU), with collective bargaining carried out at the local branch level.[33] In the US, the faculty unionisation rate is 25% in four-year public institutions,[34] but only 7% in private colleges and universities.[35] This skewed result is explained by public university coverage under state public employee collective bargaining laws, enacted in about two-thirds of the states since the 1960s.[36] Private employee rights to unionise were created in 1935 in the National Labor Relations Act (NLRA).[37] Unionisation of private university faculty was spurred in 1970, when the National Labor Relations Board (NLRB) asserted jurisdiction over non-profit private universities. However, it was brought to a standstill in 1980 when the US Supreme Court decided that most tenure-track and tenured faculty in private universities are "managerial" employees excluded from the NLRA.[38]

Another area of tension arises between the state and universities. In the UK, the state may be able to regulate widely in a way that would not be possible in the US decentralised higher education structure. Even in the US, though, the federal and state governments play an important regulatory and financing function for both public and private universities. The legitimacy of state regulation should depend on whether the state is advancing the public interest, which must include respect for the fundamental professional academic norms. For example, a state regulation requiring universities to adopt a curriculum focused on "entrepreneurship" would violate principles of institutional academic freedom and faculty academic freedom and self-governance. However, state funding to lower tuition is consistent with the democratic principles that broaden the scope of faculty academic freedom and the students' educational experience. Judicial intervention may also be appropriate to remedy the university administration's discharge of faculty members in retaliation for exercising their academic freedom in teaching, research, public speech or governance activities.

3. Contradictions of capitalism and the liberal state

In liberal democracies like the UK and US, commitment to higher education as a public good is complicated by the contradictions of building democratic institutions within a capitalist economy. Since the emergence of the modern university in the late nineteenth and early twentieth centuries, private economic interests have influenced the structure and mission of higher education. Even as public university systems have expanded, class interests remain deeply entrenched in maintaining the hierarchy of universities, whether along the lines of the Ivy League in the US or the Russell Group in the UK. In both cases,

[33] University and College Union (UCU), "Our History" <www.ucu.org.uk/article/2176/Our-history> accessed 11 October 2020; UCU, "Structures and Decision-Making" <www.ucu.org.uk/structures> accessed 11 October 2020.

[34] These rates are as of 2012. Joe Berry and Michelle Savarese, "Directory of Faculty Contracts and Bargaining Agents in Institutions of Higher Education" (Richard Boris ed, National Center for the Study of Collective Bargaining in Higher Education and the Professions 2012) (hereinafter "Directory of Faculty Contracts"). In public two-year college faculty members, the faculty unionisation rate was 42%.

[35] "Directory of Faculty Contracts" (n 34).

[36] Louis Shedd, Stephen G Katsinas and Nathaniel Bray, "Examining the Employment Profile of Institutions Under the Mission-Driven Classification System and the Impact of Collective Bargaining" (2020) 11(5) Journal of Collective Bargaining in the Academy 1, 11–12 <https://thekeep.eiu.edu/jcba/vol11/iss1/5> accessed 11 October 2020.

[37] 1935 49 Stat 449, codified at 29 USC §§ 151–169.

[38] *National Labor Relations Board v Yeshiva University*, 444 US 672 (1980).

the "top tiers" of universities perpetuate the class structure by preparing the economic and political elite to dominate political, economic, and educational institutions. Yet the widespread agreement that higher education has a public mission reveals the potential to build democratic institutions. In this way, public education is similar to other public goods, such as national health insurance, publicly subsidised housing, and paid parental leave. Education, though, has a unique revolutionary potential to change the status quo through teaching, learning, and research that question current social, political, and economic arrangements. As US Supreme Court Justice Oliver Wendell Holmes stated, "Every idea is an incitement."[39] In the communal culture of the university, individuals may be incited to build on others' ideas in contributing to the public domain of knowledge across the range of academic disciplines, all of which will be available to individuals, organisations, and institutions outside the university.

It is essential to preserve the university's public mission, even while recognising the flaws and contradictions of current higher education systems. Similar to other types of social change, higher education was democratised through organised demands for faculty academic freedom and broad public access to education. Maintaining and expanding these advances, however, remains contingent on state and institutional commitment to democratic values of higher education. As social and political conditions have changed since the 1980s ascendance of neoliberalism, however, the institutional vulnerability of higher education has become apparent.

II. The vulnerable university: corporatisation vs. the public interest

The rise of neoliberalism since the 1980s has had enormous impacts in the UK and the US, as the ideological vision of the superiority of market relations has dominated state policy and practice.[40] Central to neoliberalism is privatisation, which is justified as a means of shrinking "big government" by shifting public functions, from education to healthcare, to private for-profit businesses.[41] The label of "privatisation", however, obscures the reality of the ongoing role of the state, which remains active by subsidising corporate wealth and power.[42] As Professor Fineman observes, "Entities such as corporations, schools, workplaces, families, or churches are legitimated and given a status that confers on them benefits and protections by law. Their very content and meaning is defined through state processes. The dissolution of many of these entities is also accomplished only through state processes."[43]

A. Privatisation and commodification of higher education

In the UK and US, neoliberal ideology and privatisation trends have undermined higher education's institutional public mission through changes in funding and in

---

[39] *Gitlow v NY*, 268 US 652, 673 (1925).

[40] See Martha Albertson Fineman, "Vulnerability and Social Justice" (2019) 53 Valparaiso University Law Review 341, 347–50.

[41] Jody Freeman and Martha Minow (eds), *Government by Contract: Outsourcing and American Democracy* (Harvard University Press 2009).

[42] See Jesse Drucker and Jim Tankersley, "How Big Companies Won New Tax Breaks From the Trump Administration" *New York Times* (31 December 2019) A1.

[43] Martha Albertson Fineman, "The Vulnerable Subject and the Responsive State" (2010) 60 Emory LJ 251, 272; see also, Martha Albertson Fineman, "Vulnerability and Social Justice" (2019) 53 Valparaiso University Law Review 341, 364–67.

university form and functions. Often referred to as "corporatisation", these structural changes apply a corporate model to define the institutional identity of the university as a market actor. Although the scale and the means may differ in some instances, it is striking how similar and pervasive these institutional changes are in both countries.

At the core of privatisation in higher education are deep cuts in public funding, which have uneven financial effects on the institutions, depending on their ability to replace public funding. Regardless of a university's ability to fill the gap through other sources, the state sends the ideological message that higher education is not a public good, but rather, is one of many goods and services that can be purchased in the private market. With the commodification of higher education come cascading effects that alter the identities of those within the institution, treating students as consumers of education, and faculty as expendable labour.[44] Viewing education as a commodity justifies substituting higher tuition and student loans for public resources, as the UK Conservative government did in 2011, following budget cuts in public funding for teaching.[45] In the US, public and private universities have raised tuition, which creates severe financial impediments for middle class and working class students, with particularly negative impacts on students of colour.[46]

In the US and UK, states tout rising tuition as a way to place individual responsibility on students to decide whether their education is worth investing in student loans, extra jobs, or both.[47] The UK 2011 White Paper is particularly cynical, stating that the tuition system "put[s] financial power into the hands of learners".[48] What students will learn, however, is that financial pressures point them towards a major leading to lucrative employment in fields such as finance and engineering.[49] The UK funding cuts for teaching favoured this approach, as public funding will support only certain subjects, "such as Medicine, Science, and Engineering".[50] In both countries, the governments have legitimised and publicly subsidised for-profit education through student loans and grants.[51]

---

44 Risa L Lieberwitz, "Faculty in the Corporate University: Professional Identity, Law, and Collective Action" (2007) 16 Cornell Journal of Law and Public Policy 263.

45 Department for Business Innovation and Skills, *Students at the Heart of the System* (Cm 8122, 2011) 83.

46 Christopher Newfield, *The Great Mistake* (Johns Hopkins University Press 2016) 278–82; Michael Mitchell, Michael Leachman and Matt Saenz, "State Higher Education Funding Cuts Have Pushed Costs to Students, Worsened Inequality" (Center on Budget and Policy Priorities, 24 October 2019) 9–15.

47 Christopher Newfield, *The Great Mistake* (Johns Hopkins University Press 2016) 190–222.

48 Department for Business Innovation and Skills, *Students at the Heart of the System* (Cm 8122, 2011) 5.

49 Wendy Brown, *Undoing the Demos* (Zone Books 2015) 182–83.

50 Department for Business Innovation and Skills, *Students at the Heart of the System* (Cm 8122, 2011) 8. In responding to the White Paper, the University and College Union, "Students at the Heart of the System, Higher Education White Paper: UCU Response" (2011) 1 explained its opposition to "the overall strategy in the White Paper which seeks ultimately to privatise higher education by shifting its funding from the state to individual students and their families. This represents an impoverished view of the purposes of higher education and poses a fundamental threat to its ability to meet the wider social, cultural and economic needs of the country" <www.ucu.org.uk/article/1865/Site-search?q=students+at+the+heart&go=search> accessed 25 January 2021.

51 Osamudia R James, "Predatory Ed: The Conflict Between Public Good and For-Profit Higher Education" (2011) 38 JC & UL 45; Jonathan White, "For-Profit Higher Education in the UK: The Politics of Market Creation" in Tressie McMillan Cottom and William A Darity, Jr (eds), *For-Profit Universities: The Shifting Landscape of Marketized Higher Education* (Palgrave Macmillan 2017).

B. Privatising and commercialising academic research

Academic research has been commodified in the US and UK, promoted by national policy to encourage universities to profit from marketing academic research and to develop closer relationships with industry. In the US, federal legislation enacted in 1980 permits and encourages universities to patent federally funded research discoveries and license the patents, including exclusive licences to for-profit corporations.[52] This reverses the norm of placing publicly funded research results in the public domain.[53] The legislation triggered an explosion of university technology transfer offices to promote the patenting and licensing of academic research.[54] Corporate funding of academic research in public and private universities has also grown, including large-scale funding in exchange for exclusive licences to patents on resulting academic research.[55] Many individual faculty members have relationships with industry, either through university research contracts or faculty consulting.[56]

In the UK, the state has integrated changes in the public funding process with the commercialisation of academic research. The state's Research Assessment Exercise (RAE) and its successor Research Excellence Framework (REF) replaced the block grant system of allocating public research funds.[57] Beginning in 1986, the RAE allocated public research funding to universities based on a numerical rating system of research quality, as judged by national review panels of faculty appointed by the governmental Higher Education Funding Council for England (HEFCE).[58]

In 2002, the state created the Research Councils UK (RCUK) as "the strategic partnership of the UK's seven Research Councils", encouraging businesses to benefit from the annual £3 billion in public funds that the Research Councils distribute to academic

---

[52]Bayh-Dole Act of 1980 (Patent and Trademark Law Amendments Act) Pub L 96-517, 12 December 1980), 94 Stat 3015, codified as amended at 35 USC §§200–212.

[53]Rebecca S Eisenberg, "Public Research and Private Development: Patents and Technology Transfer in Government-Sponsored Research" (1996) 82 Virginia Law Review 1663, 1675–76.

[54]Between 1988 and 2003, US patents awarded to academic institutions quadrupled, from about 800 to more than 3200 per year. Josephine Johnston, "Health Related Academic Technology Transfer: Rethinking Patenting and Licensing Practices" (2007) 9 International Journal of Biotechnology 156, 162. In 2016, 6639 patents were granted to US universities. Jon Marcus, "Think Universities Are Making Lots of Money from Inventions? Think Again" (*The Hechinger Report*, 17 January 2020) 5 <https://hechingerreport.org/think-universities-are-making-lots-of-money-from-inventions-think-again/> accessed 11 October 2020.

[55]American Association of University Professors, "Recommended Principles & Practices to Guide Academic-Industry Relationships" (AAUP Foundation 2014) 39–47, 65–67 (hereinafter "AAUP Recommended Principles") <www.aaup.org/report/recommended-principles-practices-guide-academy-industry-relationships> accessed 11 October 2020; Risa L Lieberwitz, "Faculty in the Corporate University: Professional Identity, Law, and Collective Action" (2007) 16 Cornell Journal of Law and Public Policy 263, 310–18. By one estimate, between 1985 and 2005 corporate funding for university research increased by 250%, from $950 million to $2.4 billion. Joachin Palomino, "Billions of Corporate Dollars Are Hijacking University Research to Help Make Profits" (*Alternet*, 22 April 2013) <www.alternet.org/2013/04/billions-corporate-dollars-are-hijacking-university-research-help-make-profits/> accessed 11 October 2020.

[56]David Blumenthal, "Biotech in Northeast Ohio Conference: Conflict of Interest in Biomedical Research" (2002) 12 Health Matrix 377, 379; David Blumenthal and others, "Relationships Between Academic Institutions and Industry in the Life Sciences – An Industry Survey" (1996) 334 New England Journal of Medicine 368,371–72.

[57]There were six rounds of the RAE, in 1986, 1989, 1992, 1996, 2001, and 2008, followed by one round of the REF in 2014, with the next REF round scheduled for 2021.

[58]Since 1986, the proportion of research funds allocated under the RAE increased from 10% to 30% in 1989 and 100% in 1992. David Harvie, "Alienation, Class and Enclosure in UK Universities" (2000) 24 Capital and Class 103, 109–10, citing Henry Miller, *The Management of Change in Universities: Universities, State and Economy in Australia, Canada and the United Kingdom* (Society for Research into Higher Education 1995). In April 2018, HEFCE closed and was replaced by UK Research and Innovation (UKRI) and the Office for Students (OfS) <www.gov.uk/government/organisations/higher-education-funding-council-for-england> accessed 25 January 2021.

research.[59] In 2017, the RCUK was replaced by the UK Research and Innovation (UKRI), to bring together the Research Councils, Innovate UK, and Research England.[60]

The REF added an assessment criterion of the "impact" of the research on the business, non-profit and public sectors.[61] Since 2002, UK national policy, however, has prioritised "knowledge exchange" from academia to business. The 2003 Lambert review recommended government policies to encourage further technology transfer, including increased public funding of fundamental science research that businesses can then commercialise.[62] A 2004 Treasury Report refers approvingly to HEFCE's commitment that "membership of panels and sub-panels [of the 2008 RAE] will include people with experience of commissioning and using research, including industry and commerce".[63]

Law and policy supporting commercialisation of academic research use tactics of cooptation and coercion to achieve deep changes in relationships, culture and the institutional mission of higher education. Whether states use incentives or regulatory requirements to recast academic research as marketable products and transactions, the negative effects on academic freedom, communalism, and institutional goals are the same. As Colley observes about the impact criterion under the REF, this "is a crucial issue of academic freedom" as it creates a norm "shaped by political and administrative interests, not only pronouncing on the quality of research, but also deciding what research can be funded", which ultimately affects what research will be done.[64]

Academic freedom depends on faculty autonomy to engage in research without conflicts of interest, whether these are personal economic interests or those of the university and industry. This basic tenet protects against confounding influences that could undermine the quality of the research and the public trust in the results. The communal culture of academia is based on the value of sharing research data, process, and results in the public domain to enable others to test the research validity. It also

[59] See Risa L Lieberwitz, "Privatizing and Corporatizing the University: A U.S. and UK Comparison" in Martha Albertson Fineman, Titti Mattsson and Ulrika Andersson (eds), *Privatization, Vulnerability, And Social Responsibility: A Comparative Perspective* (Routledge 2017) 143–60, discussing the RCUK report, *Research and Business: A Productive Partnership* <https://webarchive.nationalarchives.gov.uk/20170714125540/http://www.rcuk.ac.uk/publications/reports/research-and-business-a-productive-partnership/> accessed 25 January 2021. See also, the Wilson report, "A Review of Business University Collaboration" (2012), which aims at recognising and developing "[u]niversities [as] an integral part of the supply chain to business – a supply chain that has the capability to support business growth and therefore economic prosperity". Tim Wilson, "A Review of Business–University Collaboration" (Report, February 2012) 2, p 1 <www.gov.uk/government/uploads/system/uploads/attachment_data/file/32383/12-610-wilson-review-business-university-collaboration.pdf> accessed 12 October 2020. See UKRI, "Working with Business" <https://webarchive.nationalarchives.gov.uk/20200814181612/https://www.ukri.org/innovation/working-with-business/> accessed 25 January 2021.

[60] UK Research and Innovation (UKRI), "About Us" <www.ukri.org/about-us/>; UKRI, "Working with Business" <https://webarchive.nationalarchives.gov.uk/20200814181612/https://www.ukri.org/innovation/working-with-business/> accessed 25 January 2021.

[61] Higher Education Funding Council for Englnd (HEFCE), REF2014, "Assessment Framework and Guidance on Submissions" (July 2011) <www.ref.ac.uk/2014/pubs/2011-02/> accessed 12 October 2020. The 2014 REF accorded 20% of the assessment of research to impact, to be increased to 25% in 2021. HEFCE, REF2021, "Index of Revisions to the 'Panel Criteria and Working Methods' (2019/02)" (October 2020) <www.ref.ac.uk/publications/panel-criteria-and-working-methods-201902/> accessed 12 October 2020; HEFCE, REF2014, "Decisions on Assessing Research Impact" (2011 March) <www.ref.ac.uk/2014/pubs/2011-01/> accessed 12 October 2020.

[62] Richard Lambert, "Lambert Review of Business-University Collaboration, Final Report" (report to HM Treasury, December 2003) <www.ncub.co.uk/reports/lambert-review.html> accessed 12 October 2020.

[63] HM Treasury, "Science & Innovation Investment Framework 2004-2014" (July 2004) 174.

[64] Helen Colley, "What (a) to Do about 'Impact': A Bourdieusian Critique" (2014) 4 British Educational Research Journal 660, 676, citing Judith Butler, "Academic Norms, Contemporary Challenges: A Reply to Robert Post on Academic Freedom" in B Doumani (ed), *Academic Freedom after September 11* (Zone Books 2006).

recognises the collective nature of building on others' ideas and knowledge, as expressed by Isaac Newton, that he stands "on the shoulders of giants".[65] In 1955, when asked who owned his polio vaccine, Dr Jonas Salk is quoted as responding, "Well, the people, I would say. There is no patent. Could you patent the sun?"[66]

The collective and communal nature of academic research is consistent with the state's role in providing resources to higher education institutions to encourage faculty researchers to share their data, methods, and findings with colleagues, students, and the public. This creates vibrant and resilient institutions that are part of a broader endeavour to advance knowledge and reproduce these relationships for the future. In contrast, incentives or requirements conditioned on privatisation and technology transfer to industry encourage an individualistic and transactional approach to academic research, as if faculty were working for the research and development department of for-profit corporations. Negative impacts on academic research include increased secrecy in research, delays in publishing research results,[67] bias in faculty research funded by corporations,[68] and corporate pressure on faculty to change research reports.[69]

C. Undermining academic freedom and tenure with a contingent faculty workforce

University corporatisation imports a corporate labour model that facilitates the commodification of teaching and research. In both the US and UK, the model expands the layers of university administrators, while replacing tenure-track/tenured or permanent faculty lines with a largely contingent workforce. In the US, in the period between 1976 and 2015, the number of full-time executives and managers grew by 140%, while full-time faculty grew by 86%.[70] The national rate of tenure-track/tenured faculty positions has been reversed, from 78% in 1969 to the current level of 30%.[71] In the UK, there are similar trends of increased top-down management[72] and decreased faculty job security.

[65] Lawrence M Sung, "Collegiality and Collaboration in the Age of Exclusivity" (2000) 3 DePaul Journal of Health Care Law 411, 417 fn 17, 436–38 (citing Robert Merton, *On the Shoulders of Giants: A Shandean Postscript* (1965) 31 fn 3 (quoting Letter from Sir Isaac Newton to Robert Hooke (5 Feb 1675 or 1676).

[66] Douglas M Birch and Gary Cohn, "Standing Up to Industry: As Corporations Increasingly Hold Their Purse Strings, Many Researchers Feel Pressed to Deliver Favorable Results" *Baltimore Sun* (26 June 2001) 1A.

[67] Martin Kenney, *Biotechnology: The University-Industrial Complex* (Yale University Press 1986) 108–11; Jonathan King and Doreen Stabinsky, "Patents on Cells, Genes, and Organisms Undermine the Exchange of Scientific Ideas" *Chronicle of Higher Education* (9 February 1999) D6.

[68] "AAUP Recommended Principles" (n 55) 88–91; Sheldon Krimsky, *Science in the Private Interest: Has the Lure of Profits Corrupted Biomedical Research?* (Rowman & Littlefield Publishers 2003) 142–49.

[69] "AAUP Recommended Principles" (n 55) 60–76.

[70] Thomas D Snyder and Charlene M Hoffman, "Digest of Education Statistics 2001" (National Center for Education Statistics 2002) table 224; Thomas D Snyder, Cristobal de Brey and Sally A Dillow, "Digest of Education Statistics" (52nd edn 2016, National Center for Education Statistics 2018) tables 314.20, 314.30; AAUP, "The Annual Report on the Economic Status of the Profession, 2013-14" <www.aaup.org/our-work/research/annual-report-economic-status-profession> accessed 12 October 2020; AAUP, "Visualizing Change: The Annual Report on the Economic Status of the Profession, 2016-17" <www.aaup.org/our-work/research/FCS> accessed 12 October 2020.

[71] AAUP, "Visualizing Change: The Annual Report on the Economic Status of the Profession, 2016-17" <www.aaup.org/our-work/research/FCS> accessed 12 October 2020; Ernst Benjamin, "The Eroding Foundations of Academic Freedom and Professional Integrity: Implications of the Diminishing Proportion of Tenured Faculty for Organizational Effectiveness in Higher Education" (2010) 1 AAUP Journal of Academic Freedom, p 4 <www.aaup.org/reports-publications/journal-academic-freedom/volume-1> accessed 25 January 2021.

[72] Rosemary Deem, "The Knowledge Worker, the Manager-Academic and the Contemporary UK University: New and Old Forms of Public Management?" (2004) 20 Financial Accountability & Management 107.

Between 2007/08 and 2017/18, academic staff in higher education increased by 23%, while the proportion on "traditional lecturer" (teaching and research) contracts fell below 50% for the first time, with these changes having a disproportionately negative impact on women and ethnic minorities. In 2017/18, 67% of researchers and 49% of teaching-only staff were on fixed-term contracts, with 42% of the teaching-only staff on hourly paid contracts.[73] This employment model has serious gender and racial impacts, as the shrinking percentage of permanent or tenure-track faculty lines creates institutional obstacles to hiring and promoting women and people of colour into faculty positions with strong job security.[74]

The restructuring of the employment model changes the nature of institutional power and relationships, imposing a top-down system of unilateral decision-making about academic programmes and faculty labour issues. In the UK, the bureaucratic layers are even more complex due to the cumbersome national agencies linked to the REF and assessment under the more recently launched 2016 Teaching Excellence Framework (TEF).[75] This hierarchical decision-making structure is antithetical to faculty academic freedom and self-governance. Moreover, the multiple aspects of commodification and commercialisation of higher education are interrelated and self-reinforcing. A largely contingent faculty workforce has weakened collective power to demand reinstatement of professional norms of academic freedom, tenure, and shared governance.

The growth in contingent faculty labour increases stratification and creates obstacles to building faculty unity. In both the US and UK, divisions among faculty positions are defined not only by differences in job security, but also in the nature of the work. In the US, tenure-track/tenured faculty continue to engage in both teaching and research, consistent with the traditional understanding that they are mutually beneficial. However, the labour of non-tenure-track faculty is commodified by categorising them as either teachers or researchers.[76] In the UK, the RAE and REF distinction between "research-active" and "research-inactive" faculty has stratified permanent faculty

---

[73] UCU, "Precarious Work in Higher Education: Insecure Contracts and How They Have Changed Over Time" (Report, May 2020) 15–18, 22, 26 <www.ucu.org.uk/article/1865/Site-search?q=Precarious+Work+in+Higher+Education> accessed 12 October 2020; Nick Megoran and Olivia Mason, "Second Class Academic Citizens: The Dehumanising Effects of Casualisation in Higher Education" (University and College Union Report, January 2020) 6 <www.ucu.org.uk/article/1865/Site-search?q=Second+Class+Academic+Citizens> accessed 12 October 2020.

[74] Ernst Benjamin, "The Eroding Foundations of Academic Freedom and Professional Integrity: Implications of the Diminishing Proportion of Tenured Faculty for Organizational Effectiveness in Higher Education" (2010) 1 AAUP Journal of Academic Freedom, pp 6–7 <www.aaup.org/reports-publications/journal-academic-freedom/volume-1> accessed 25 January 2021; Peter Halewood and Donna Young, "Rule of Law, Activism, and Equality: Growing Antisubordination Norms within the Neoliberal University" (2017) 50 John Marshall Law Review 249, 255–56; UCU, "Precarious Work in Higher Education: Insecure Contracts and How They Have Changed Over Time" (Report, May 2020) 15–18, 22, 26 <www.ucu.org.uk/article/1865/Site-search?q=Precarious+Work+in+Higher+Education> accessed 12 October 2020.

[75] Liz Morrish, "The Accident of Accessibility: How the Data of the TEF Creates Neoliberal Subjects" (2019) 33 Social Epistemology 355; Matt O'Leary, Dr Vanessa Cui and Dr Amanda French, "Understanding, Recognising and Rewarding Teaching Quality in Higher Education: An Exploration of the Impact and Implications of the Teaching Excellence Framework" (Project report for the University and College Union, February 2019) <www.ucu.org.uk/article/1865/Site-search?q=tef&go=search> accessed 12 October 2020.

[76] John C Duncan, Jr, "The Indentured Servants of Academia: The Adjunct Faculty Dilemma and Their Limited Legal Remedies" (1999) 74 Indiana Law Journal 513, 524–28; Coalition for the Academic Workforce, "A Portrait of Part-Time Faculty Members: A Summary of Findings on Part-Time Faculty Respondents to the Coalition on the Academic Workforce Survey of Contingent Faculty Members and Instructors" (Report, June 2012) <www.academicworkforce.org/survey.html> accessed 12 October 2020.

positions, as well. Such divisions are destructive to the communal culture of the university by creating a second-class status that excludes faculty from being fully integrated members of the university.[77]

III. The future of the vulnerable university

Given the totalising nature of neoliberalism that has taken hold since the 1980s, it is not surprising that it has affected higher education institutions in the US and UK. What is striking is the pervasive and interlocking nature of the institutional changes that have severely undermined the public mission of the university, and indeed, the notion of higher education as a public good. Perhaps most striking is the extent to which higher education institutions have internalised the neoliberal agenda. Thus, what began as external political influences, through a combination of public policy incentives and regulations, have been embraced by universities as their raison d'être.

State funding of the "massification" of public higher education in the 1960s responded to public needs and desires for higher education during a time of social and political activism on and off campus. The progressive changes during this period strengthened the institutional role of higher education to serve the public interest by providing access to a more diverse student population and by increasing the ranks of faculty with academic freedom to bring new ideas to teaching and research across a broad range of disciplines. These conditions also created the foundation for conflicts, with student activism in social justice movements leading to mass demonstrations, campus strikes, and demands for democratic participation in campus governance. Campus activism affected faculty, with divisions between faculty engaging in social activism and faculty resisting challenges to their authority.

Through the lens of vulnerability theory, the growth of public higher education in the 1960s can be seen as a positive process of building strong and resilient institutions in the public interest. The state's distribution of resources to expand public higher education democratised the existing system of universities that had been open only to the economic and political elite. Building this higher education system is also consistent with retaining democratic principles of faculty academic freedom, job security, and self-governance, which provide faculty with independence from the administration and the state. Considered together, the state's support for public universities and the internal academic labour structure create the conditions for an educational system that can grow and change over time, responding to new ideas and challenges to the status quo in academic disciplines and in university structures. Conflict inside and outside the classroom and research settings is an intrinsic part of this process. The responsive state thus recognises that democratic higher education institutions, with all the debate, disruption, and turmoil that go with them, are essential to the social reproduction of an educational system that serves the public interest.

The 1960s state support for public higher education was successful in important ways. A broader and more diverse student population benefited personally and professionally from their university education. Many students of the 1960s and 1970s graduated with a commitment to social justice and public service, which influenced their career choices

---

[77]Lisa Lucas, *The Research Game in Academic Life* (Open University Press 2006) 44. Hugh Willmott, "Commercialising Higher Education in the UK: The State, Industry and Peer Review" (2003) 28 Studies in Higher Education 129, 134–35, 139.

and public engagement. Children of first generation graduates could more easily follow a path to higher education. Students who continued on to graduate studies influenced the universities as future members of the faculty, bringing new perspectives that challenged established approaches to pedagogy, academic disciplines, and university governance.

State commitment to higher education as a public good has always been partial, however, given the contradictions of democratic institutions existing within a capitalist economy. The progress made in the 1960s, while meaningful, was only a brief period of democratic institutional change. Further, the success of students and faculty in challenging the status quo may have, ironically, contributed to the resurgence of conservative governmental policies in the mid to late 1970s. In the US and UK, such public policy measures have recalibrated the state's actions to emphasise the ideological vision of higher education as an engine of industry. Some policies have relied on neoliberal ideology more directly than have others. Public funding cuts and increased tuition have been justified in non-ideological terms as economic austerity measures addressing the growing costs of higher education. The impact of such measures on students, however, has been justified in overtly ideological terms, lauding the benefits of students' individual responsibility to calculate whether taking on debt will provide a positive return on investment in a university degree. However, this ignores the state's abdication of its social obligation to provide equal access to higher education. By shifting state responsibility to individual students to go into debt to pay high tuition, the state undermines their autonomy by restricting access to higher education while also placing financial pressures on students to pursue lucrative careers in business. Under vulnerability theory, the responsive state should provide public funding for equal access to higher education, which would develop students' autonomy and resilience in their personal and public lives. Further, providing higher education as a public good legitimately creates a reciprocal relationship in which students can and should apply their education to contribute to the public welfare.[78]

The state and universities' rationale for changing funding structures for academic research is also articulated in non-ideological terms, as the need to find alternative resources to cover the rising costs of higher education, including science and technology research. Through a combination of public policy incentives and coercive measures, the state has redirected universities and faculty to fill the funding gaps by establishing relationships with business and industry. University–industry relationships seek more than funding, though. Rather, they create ongoing symbiotic institutional relationships[79] based on their ideological alignment in support of a shared goal of commercialising academic research. The more successful these relationships in privatising academic research, the more the state can justify further public funding cuts.

---

[78]See Martha Albertson Fineman, "The Vulnerable Subject and the Responsive State" (2010) 60 Emory LJ 251, 260–61: "If, however, we were to start our discussion of what is the proper relationship between state and individual with the primary objective being that of ensuring and enhancing a meaningful equality of opportunity and access, we may see a need for a more active and responsive state. This would not mean casting aside autonomy, but rather that we realize that as desirable as autonomy is as an aspiration, it cannot be attained without an underlying provision of substantial assistance, subsidy, and support from society and its institutions, which give individuals the resources they need to create options and make choices .... Nor should autonomy be confused with isolation or separation from society. Part of the reciprocity inherent in being a member of society is that everyone has a role to play in ensuring the greater good."

[79]For a discussion of the way in which symbiotic relationships between institutions should work for the public good, based on vulnerability theory, see Martha Albertson Fineman, "Universality, Vulnerability, and Collective Responsibility" (forthcoming in *Les ateliers de l'éthique/The Ethics Forum*).

Policies encouraging commercialisation of academic research do not directly interfere with faculty academic freedom. Many individual faculty view relationships with industry as providing opportunities to fund their research agendas and to share in the profits flowing from royalties and licensing. However, such "incentives" are a means of cooptation that shift the mission of university research from serving the public to serving private interests. This harms academic research, faculty professional norms, and the broader public. Faculty are encouraged to narrow their research agendas to search for short-term results that can be patented and licensed. This is antithetical to the academic research process, which develops basic and applied research agendas based on intellectual curiosity, information gathered through trial and error, and unexpected discoveries. The professional norms of communalism and the public domain of research express the reciprocal relationships of trust among faculty and between the university and the public. The commercial research process, however, undermines faculty collegial relationships and public trust in academic research.

Similar to the stated rationales for changing funding models for tuition and academic research, institutions of higher education seek to justify the contingent faculty model as a necessary response to funding cuts and rising costs. The reality of this labour model, however, undermines fundamental professional norms of academic freedom and faculty self-governance. The stratification of faculty with and without job security encourages exploitation of those assigned to teaching or research positions, along with unequal salaries and working conditions. The UK's RAE and the REF formalise divisions between research-active and non-research-active faculty. Again, these results are tied to the state's abdication of its responsibility to provide resources for higher education as a public good, which includes faculty employment conditions of academic freedom and job security.

The combined effect of the state's imposition of neoliberal policies and universities' embrace of the neoliberal agenda has altered higher education, redefining its institutional public mission as being equivalent to the private interests of market actors. The shift to serving corporate interests does more than simply shift institutional priorities. Rather, these changes reveal the vulnerability of institutions of higher education to changes in state regulation and policies that shift resources from advancing the public interest to supporting neoliberal privatisation agendas. As Professor Fineman observes, "[S]ocietal institutions can ameliorate or complicate our [individual] vulnerability, but they should also be understood as vulnerable entities in and of themselves … . Even the most established institutions viewed over time are potentially unstable and susceptible to challenges from both internal and external forces."[80] Aligning university interests with corporate interests undermines the institutional role of higher education to contribute to society as a whole. It also weakens universities' ability to withstand or resist further state coercive measures that compromise university independence, academic freedom, and public access to higher education.

The tragedy of the corporatised university is that its embrace of the neoliberal agenda has made it more vulnerable to external attacks on the fundamental values of higher education. In the US, the Trump administration furthered its agenda of economic inequality and corporate power by declaring war on intellectuals, labour rights, and social justice movements.[81] Under Trump, the federal government's actions during the Covid-19

[80]Martha Albertson Fineman, "The Vulnerable Subject and the Responsive State" (2010) 60 Emory LJ 251, 273.
[81]Risa L Lieberwitz, "Fighting for Our Rights Today, Building Our Strength for Tomorrow" (2019) 105(1) Academe 8 <www.aaup.org/article/fighting-our-rights-today-building-our-strength-tomorrow#.X4e4WOd7mdY> accessed 14 October 2020.

pandemic illustrate each of these attacks on progressive groups and institutions. The Trump administration rejected the validity of science as a basis for policy-making in addressing the pandemic.[82] Federal agencies charged with protecting labour narrowed worker rights to speak out about working conditions and refused to mandate safety protections in response to the pandemic.[83] Trump issued an Executive Order prohibiting the federal government, its contractors, and grantees, from engaging in diversity training regarding racial and gender biases.[84] The Trump administration imposed its anti-immigration policy in ways that undermine universities' ability to protect Deferred Action for Childhood Arrivals (DACA) students.[85] While these examples come from the extreme and polarised politics of the US, the institutional vulnerability of higher education is similar in the UK. Having adopted wholesale the individualistic and competitive ethos of the RAE and the REF, the contingency of the academic profession, and opportunity to raise tuition rates, UK universities are in a weakened position to respond to the ravages of Brexit, anti-immigration policies, and mistrust or hostility from the public.[86]

Even in the corporatised university, the progressive forces under attack are still well represented in academic programmes, student movements, and faculty unions and professional organisations. However, the institutional power of the university has been severely weakened by external cuts and self-inflicted wounds. Having failed to fight back against the drop in public funding and having embraced the privatised model of higher education, the university itself has changed. The university has compromised its independence from political and economic interests, has commercialised academic research, and has adopted a corporate model of employment precarity. It is now more difficult for the university to stand for principles of the public interest in academic freedom and public goods, including higher education, labour rights, health, and safety.

This dismal picture should not lead to despair. Rather, current political and economic conditions have drawn back the curtain to reveal the harm resulting from state policies and institutional changes that increase inequalities in wealth and power. The resilience and integrity of public interest institutions can be renewed from the ground up through organising by those who are subject to state and institutional power. Progressive social change comes through social movements that organise, build alliances, and demand that the state provide for the public welfare. This is true at the darkest moments in history and it

---

82 Katelyn Weisbrod, "6 Ways Trump's Denial of Science Has Delayed the Response to COVID-19 (and Climate Change)" (*Inside Climate News*, 19 March 2020) <https://insideclimatenews.org/news/19032020/denial-climate-change-coronavirus-donald-trump> accessed 14 October 2020.

83 Hassan A Kanu, "NLRB's GM Ruling Gives Employers More Slack to Punish Speech" (*Bloomberg Law Daily Labor Report*, 21 July 2020); Deborah Berkowitz, "Worker Safety & Health During COVID-19 Pandemic: Rights & Resources" (*National Employment Law Project*, 9 April 2020) <www.nelp.org/publication/worker-safety-health-during-covid-19-pandemic-rights-resources/> accessed 14 October 2020.

84 Hailey Fuchs, "Trump Attack on Diversity Training Has a Quick and Chilling Effect" *New York Times* (13 October 2020) <www.nytimes.com/2020/10/13/us/politics/trump-diversity-training-race.html> accessed 14 October 2020.

85 "Trump Administration Follows Up Supreme Court Defeat by 'Reconsidering' DACA Program, Keeping Thousands in Uncertainty" (*National Immigrant Justice Law Center*, 28 July 2020) <https://immigrantjustice.org/press-releases/trump-administration-follows-supreme-court-defeat-reconsidering-daca-program-keeping> accessed 14 October 2020.

86 "UCU Tells MPs that Brexit and Anti-Immigration Rhetoric Are Damaging UK Higher Education" (*University and College Union*, 25 January 2017) <www.ucu.org.uk/article/8603/UCU-tells-MPs-that-Brexit-and-anti-immigration-rhetoric-are-damaging-UK-higher-education> accessed 14 October 2020; David Matthews, "Brexit Would Be a Victory for Those Who Distrust Academics" (*Times Higher Education Blog*, 22 June 2016) <www.timeshighereducation.com/blog/brexit-would-be-victory-those-who-distrust-academics> accessed 14 October 2020; Benjamin Mueller, "'It Really Was Abandonment': Virus Crisis Grips British Universities" *New York Times* (6 October 2020) <www.nytimes.com/2020/10/06/world/europe/virus-UK-universities.html> accessed 14 October 2020.

is true in better times. In describing the role of organisations to build institutional resilience, Professor Fineman explains, "One implication of recognizing institutional vulnerability should be acceptance of the need for monitoring, evaluating, updating, and reforming our societal institutions when necessary. These processes should be undertaken consistent with the mandate of equality of access and opportunity and the obligation of the state to act with equal regard for the vulnerability of all."[87] In higher education, this means that faculty, students, and staff must join and become active in unions and other professional and social justice organisations to demand institutional change. This will not be easy, particularly for faculty who have benefited from the stratified employment system in the corporatised university. Many faculty members, however, remain committed to exercising individual academic freedom in ways that honour the collective values of the academic profession in service of the public interest. Higher education as a public good provides mutual benefits to the faculty, students, and society. Reconnecting with the intrinsic pleasure of academic work as a public good is one way to renew individual and collective resilience and solidarity among faculty and students. Bringing that energy and commitment to faculty and student unions and other social justice organisations will fuel their institutional resilience and power to demand social change in the public interest.

Disclosure statement

No potential conflict of interest was reported by the author.

[87]Martha Albertson Fineman, "The Vulnerable Subject and the Responsive State" (2010) 60 Emory LJ 251, 273.

Undermining resilience: how the modern UK university manufactures heightened vulnerability in legal academics and what is to be done

Graham Ferris

ABSTRACT

Legal academics are vulnerable and the contemporary law school is eroding their resilience. Using vulnerability theory, as developed by Professor Martha Albertson Fineman, this article analyses the reasons for the loss of assets that could provide resilience in the modern university and the modern law school. Audit culture, the economics of resourcing higher education, the growth of mass higher education, the ideology of neoliberalism, and managerialism as a feature of that ideology, are all factors that play a role in degrading the resilience of academics. The growth of precarious labour, overwork, attacks upon educational and disciplinary values, attacks upon academic freedom, and pressure on academic identity are all consequences of these factors. Disengagement, feelings of failure, ill health and low wellbeing are the embodiments of these consequences. Vulnerability theory is used to carry out a synthesis of materials drawn from literatures on education, legal education, higher education, health and safety at work, self-determination theory, and professional vocation. This synthesis highlights value conflicts between neoliberal managerialism and educational values that risk undermining academic existential resources. Vulnerability theory is then used to identify potential means of resistance and potential places for resistance within and beyond the law school.

Academics – privileged yet still (and increasingly) vulnerable

Although everyone is vulnerable, it is clearly the case that some people are less able to recover from setbacks because they have fewer resources that they can call upon in a crisis. When Mathew Miller, son of Jonathan Miller, failed to perform in his A levels he could fall back upon the social networks he inherited from his famous father.[1] Mathew Miller went on to have a successful career in the creative industries. When an accident broke a hand and leg of a poor man in Somaliland:[2]

---

[1]Aida Edemariam, "*Gloucester Crescent* by William Miller Review" *The Guardian* (London, 24 August 2018) <https://www.theguardian.com/books/2018/aug/24/gloucester-crescent-by-william-miller-review-my-dad-jonathan-miller-and-me> accessed 12 March 2021; Amanda Craig, "*Gloucester Crescent* by William Miller Review" *The Guardian* (London, 26 August 2018) <https://www.theguardian.com/books/2018/aug/26/gloucester-crescent-me-my-dad-other-grown-ups-william-miller-review> accessed 12 March 2021.

[2]Deepa Narayan and others, *Voices of the Poor: Crying Out for Change* (Oxford University Press 2000) 99, Box 5.4.

> One child died of malnutrition. Since the [the accident] he has been handicapped, and his family depends on gifts from neighbours and relatives. He has no aspirations.

A lack of money, medical care, and non-physical employment opportunities turned a serious but non-life-threatening accident into a disabling event that pitched a family into extreme poverty. The loss of good jobs, instability of personal relationships, and ready availability of opioids in the USA have fuelled a quiet demographic crisis amongst white non-Hispanic non-graduate Americans in their mid-life years, an estimated 600,000 deaths above those that would have been expected if pre-twenty-first century trends had continued into the twenty-first century.[3] A group of people in the developed world lost their way of life, had their self-respect undermined, and had a healthcare system that sold them addictive opioids for their pain.[4] These are all examples of the relationship between vulnerability and resilience, or its absence.

Sometimes vulnerability is wrongly seen as only present when there is some lack of resources or deficient character:[5]

> Vulnerability is perhaps best understood as a lack of key sets of assets, exposing individuals, households, and communities to increased or disproportionate risk of impoverishment. Simply put, an increased number and range of assets means less vulnerability.

Viewed from this perspective academics in the developed world would not be considered vulnerable as they have considerable assets, including such "key assets" as high educational levels, prestigious and fulfilling jobs, access to healthcare, healthy living environments, and relatively high rates of pay.

However, vulnerability theory as developed by Fineman rejects this approach to vulnerability, both because of its failure to take into account the human condition and because the distinction it draws between the vulnerable and those not vulnerable (or invulnerable) is untenable. In doing this she does not discard Kirby's important insight that it is people's assets that distinguish between those that are typically considered more vulnerable to adverse life events and those less vulnerable. Risk may be common, but the consequences of events are differentiated as explained by Kirby:[6]

> ... environmental hazards ... [and] many risks ... do not necessarily damage individual and social well-being if states, communities, households and individuals have adequate resources, both physical and human, to withstand them and are adequately protected by insurance cover and welfare systems ... natural disasters have a disproportionate impact upon the poor, because the poor have fewer of the resources necessary to survive and recover from such disasters.

The "risk" referred to by Kirby is risk of harm, which is vulnerability and is common to all people. People's ability to survive and respond to risk is caught by the concept of resilience. Vulnerability to harm is universal, it is part of the human condition. The ability to withstand harm is particular and determined by resources available to the person, household, institution, community, or state. Particular ability to respond to vulnerability is determined by those key assets that are available. Hence, Fineman argues vulnerability has both a universal and particular dimension and that the impact of events

---

[3]Anne Case and Angus Deaton, *Deaths of Despair and the Future of Capitalism* (Princeton University Press 2020) 32.
[4]Their somatic pain which increased as their economic and social fortunes declined, see: Anne Case and Angus Deaton, *Deaths of Despair and the Future of Capitalism* (Princeton University Press 2020) 1.
[5]Raj Patel and others, *Voices of the Poor: Can Anyone Hear Us?* (Oxford University Press 2000) 60–61.
[6]Peadar Kirby, *Vulnerability and Violence: The Impact of Globalization* (Pluto Press 2006) 54.

upon individuals and groups is determined by the degree of resilience one has, which is itself a function of available assets and life history.

These three concepts: universal vulnerability, particular positioning, and assets that provide resilience; explain why the "vulnerability as a deficiency" concept is rejected whilst retaining the vital insight that assets are crucial to resilience. These three linked concepts just provide a more realistic and fuller description of human experience. However, this is only one aspect of the rejection of the vulnerability as deficiency approach. The other aspect is the usually unarticulated counterpart to vulnerability as a deficiency which is the assumption of a default state of non-deficiency, whether we call this non-vulnerability or invulnerability. Invulnerability is more usually described as self-sufficiency or autonomy.[7] If one lacks nothing one can support oneself and live the life one chooses to live. But this independent and autonomous person, household, institution, community, or state is mythical. We are all subject to risks, we are all vulnerable, and in a modern global world those risks are often novel, inherently uncontrollable and unpredictable.[8] The invulnerable subject belongs to an unrealistic ideological world of individualism, rationality, and methodological individualism.

The state of nature imagined by John Locke and adopted by Robert Nozick is populated by pre-social individuals or households. The moral subject of Emmanuel Kant exists in a moral universe in which individual intention is everything and consequences irrelevant. The field of micro-economics is populated by economic men, rational decision-makers who are resolutely driven by self-interest and are prodigies of calculative thought.[9] All of these approaches to understanding the world rely upon creation myths (Locke and Nozick), denial of contingency (Kant), or empirically false simplifications and features (*homo economicus*). They are the intellectual foundations for classic liberal and neoliberal theory. The autonomous invulnerable individual is available as a default "common-sense" contrast to those who are vulnerable because of this ideological background. Fineman rejects this modern construct as firmly as Aristotle rejected the idea of a human without a polity.[10] This provides the other reason for framing vulnerability as universal and differences in resilience as explicable by available resources, acknowledging that variations in resources generate a particular position in regard to the ability to respond to vulnerability. As Fineman expresses it, we should substitute the "Vulnerable Subject" for the "Liberal Subject".[11]

Fineman identifies five types of assets that support resilience: physical (money, housing, transport, mobile phone); human (education, health, character); social (family, professional associations, social networks, trade unions, church or charity groups, local community relationships); ecological or environmental (clean water, healthy food, access to parks or woodland or rural environments, clean air); existential (systems of

---

[7]Martha Albertson Fineman, *The Autonomy Myth: A Theory of Dependency* (The New Press 2004).

[8]Ulrich Beck, *Risk Society: Towards a New Modernity* (Mark Ritter tr, Sage Publications 1992); Charles Perrow, *Normal Accidents: Living with High Risk Technologies* (Princeton University Press 1999); Peadar Kirby, *Vulnerability and Violence: The Impact of Globalization* (Pluto Press 2006); Ulrich Beck, *World at Risk* (Polity Press 2008).

[9]Kaushik Basu, *Prelude to Political Economy: A Study of the Social and Political Foundations of Economics* (Oxford University Press 2003) 36–64; John Kay and Mervyn King, *Radical Uncertainty: Decision Making for an Unknowable Future* (The Bridge Street Press 2020) 106–32.

[10]Aristotle, *The Politics* (TA Sinclair and Trevor J Saunders tr, Penguin Books 1992) 59–60, 1253a1-6.

[11]Martha Albertson Fineman, "Equality, Autonomy, and the Vulnerable Subject in Law and Politics" in Martha Albertson Fineman and Anna Grear (eds), *Vulnerability: Reflections on a New Ethical Foundation for Law and Politics* (Ashgate 2013) 17, 19, and 26.

meaning such as religion, caring for others, culture and art, vocation).[12] For most of these resources, the state and its institutions are crucial in their production.[13] These assets are produced by social institutions (regional or national government, markets, corporations, as well as the family). The difference between assets and institutions is analytical rather than ontological in a similar manner to the way that the categories of "institutions" and "organisations" are used in Douglass C North's work.[14] Thus, the family is a social institution at one level of analysis and a family is a social resource that can support resilience at another level of analysis. The state is pivotal because it provides the institutional structure that constitutes other institutions such as families or markets or corporations.

This brings us to our academic who is vulnerable as a human being and who works in a vulnerable organisation that is constituted and regulated by the state and operates within markets. In order to understand the particular ways in which the academic is vulnerable we need to analyse the institutional forces that are undermining resilience, whilst never forgetting that there are also institutional forces that support academic resilience. Whilst the focus in this article will be on one aspect of this shifting environment, the resilience derived from the sense of calling felt by many academics, it is important to begin by quickly sketching out some of the major institutional forces at work.

State and market stressors – the big picture

Law schools tend to form a part of a bigger organisation – the university.[15] The past 30 to 40 years have seen an expansion in the provision of higher education in the UK and internationally,[16] and they have also seen significant changes in state responsibility for the provision of higher education.[17] Many states have pulled back from direct funding of universities.[18] Funding in England is primarily derived from state loans to students and competitively awarded research grants.[19] In addition, the last 40 years have seen a

[12]Martha Albertson Fineman, "Vulnerability and Inevitable Inequality" (2017) 4 Oslo Law Review 133, 146.
[13]ibid.
[14]Douglass C North, *Institutions, Institutional Change and Economic Performance* (Cambridge University Press 1990) ch 1.
[15]Not always; in the UK one significant provider of legal education is the College of Law, which is a legal education specialist and not located in any larger university setting.
[16]Trow traces the UK transformation of higher education, in Martin Trow, "Academic Standards and Mass Higher Education" in Martin Trow, *Twentieth-Century Higher Education* (John Hopkins University Press 2010) and see: <www.oecd.org/education/higher-education-needs-to-step-up-efforts-to-prepare-students-for-the-future.htm> accessed 6 October 2019.
[17]Martin Trow, "Academic Standards and Mass Higher Education" in Trow (2010) (n 16); in the UK massification took place largely from the late 1980s and through the 1990s. This was not the case in the USA, which saw massification much earlier; see Martin Trow, "The Second Transformation of American Secondary Education" and "Federalism in American Higher Education" in Trow (2010) (n 16). However, the UK, the USA and Australia saw parallel state withdrawal of direct support, and increasing conditionality of what support was maintained, over the last 30 years; see: Ruth Barcan, *Academic Life and Labour in the New University: Hope and Other Choices* (Routledge 2016). This international phenomenon was not therefore caused by massification per se (as it did not coincide with massification across nations) and was connected to ideologies of market desirability and managerialism which are examined below.
[18]For the shifting pattern of funding in the USA see: Anne Stauffer and others, *Two Decades of Change in Federal and State Higher Education Funding* (The Pew Charitable Trusts 2019) <www.pewtrusts.org/-/media/assets/2019/10/fedstatefundinghigheredu_chartbook_v1.pdf> accessed 13 July 2020.
[19]Educational funding is devolved, the sources below are for England. Philip Augar and others, *Independent Panel Report to the Review of Post-18 Education and Funding* (Department for Education 2019) Figure 3.1 which shows the decline in per student funding over the 1990s and subsequent increases from 2005–06 and 2012 to date

widespread deployment of a "neoliberal" ideology of the market as the preferred mechanism for solving all social coordination problems.[20]

These shifts in the political and cultural sphere have coincided with a loss of consensus about the function and role of the university that is linked to both greater social and student diversity and intellectual acceptance of pluralism or relativism in the value realm.[21] The last 30 years have also seen the growth of a market-based international higher education market, an explosion of information technology, and the rise of a reductionist vision of education as the building of human capital.[22]

Some legal academics exist on short-term contracts or zero hours contracts across multiple university sites and struggle with a shortage of physical assets.[23] In the UK a PhD requires for most people an undergraduate degree, a master's degree, before pursuing a PhD degree. That is seven or eight years of post-secondary study. To end such an extended period of study in insecure work with no guarantee of career progression makes academia, including legal academia, an extremely expensive profession to enter.[24] There are persistent disparities in pay and progression for those who manage to obtain full-time employment that suggest discrimination against women and people of colour in the UK.[25] These discriminatory practices extend to other groups who do not have protected characteristics, and for whom data is not gathered.[26]

Political demands upon the university have escalated as state financial support has wavered. In societies marked by increasing inequality, universities are exhorted to

---

linked to fee increases (to £3000 in 2005 and £9000 in 2012), as noted at 63: "Undergraduate teaching after 2012 became a profitable activity and the sector responded as it was meant to by recruiting more students, improving student support and developing facilities." Government research funding is provided under the "dual support" mechanism, Higher Education Funding Council for England funding linked to REF performance by institutions and competitive grants awarded by the research councils. For funding per student between 1979 and 1996, see: Gareth Williams, "The Market Route to Mass Higher Education: British Experience 1979–1996" (1997) 10 Higher Education Policy 275.

[20] David Harvey, *A Brief History of Neoliberalism* (Oxford University Press 2007); Margaret Thornton, *Privatising the Public University: The Case of Law* (Routledge 2011). Belief in the neoliberal reform of governance programme transcends the two-party political divide, as both New Labour in the UK and the Clinton administration in the US continued the neoliberal reform agenda.

[21] R Barnett, *Thinking and Rethinking the University: The Selected Works of Ronald Barnett* (Routledge 2014); Bill Readings, *The University in Ruins* (Harvard University Press 1996); Harry Lewis, *Excellence Without a Soul: Does Liberal Education Have a Future?* (Public Affairs 2007).

[22] See eg Harry Brighouse, *On Education* (Routledge 2006) 27 and 37. Human capital theory does not adequately address positional effects of human and cultural capital, see: Pierre Bourdieu, "The Forms of Capital" in AH Halsey and others (eds), *Education: Culture, Economy, Society* (Oxford University Press 1997) 46. See: Lee Elliot Major and Stephen Machin, *Social Mobility: And Its Enemies* (Pelican 2018).

[23] UCU, "Precarious Work in Higher Education: Insecure Contracts and How They Have Changed Over Time" (May 2020); UCU, "Counting the Costs of Casualisation in Higher Education" (June 2019). MY Tytherleigh and others, "Occupational Stress in UK Higher Education Institutions: A Comparative Study of All Staff Categories" (2005) 24 Higher Education Research and Development 41 identified job insecurity as the most important cause of academic stress. David Matthews, "Don't Casualize Academics, Says OECD" *THE* (London, 29 June 2020) <https://www.timeshighereducation.com/news/dont-casualise-academics-says-oecd> accessed 12 March 2021.

[24] Primarily as a simple result of the increase in student fees and lost opportunity costs (loss of potential earning and career advancement). In the law schools, however, there is also a shift from recruiting practitioners to recruiting holders of PhDs, and this tends to increase the costs of qualification (due to higher fees and lost opportunity costs).

[25] UCU, "The Gender Pay Gap in Higher Education" (2015/16 data report); UCU, "Black Academic Staff Face Double Whammy in Promotion and Pay Stakes" <www.ucu.org.uk/article/10360/Black-academic-staff-face-double-whammy-in-promotion-and-pay-stakes> accessed 12 June 2020.

[26] See: <http://workingclassacademics.com/memberspublications/>accessed 12 June 2020.

increase social mobility.[27] In nation states which have renounced responsibility for employment levels and social security, universities are required to serve the employment market and enhance national competitiveness.[28] In an ideological context of release of government control to allow market forces to allocate resources, universities are subject to ever-increasing levels of audit.[29]

Market discipline is exulted, but pseudo-market control is imposed via "new public management" and regulation through audit.[30] New public management is a conflation of business organisation with market mechanism, the visible hand being passed off as the invisible hand.[31] The growth of managerialism undermines the sense of meaning many academics try to find in their work, in the words of Shattock:[32]

> For many academics this marked a significant change in their relationship to their institution from being a member to being an employee, from being a partner in an enterprise to being someone whose performance could be measured by remote internal and external bureaucracies. This constituted a negation of the individual autonomy of the professional.[33]

It is important to explore the consequences of these institutional power shifts, which have been driven by government policies, on individual academics.

In short managing a university is a nightmarish prospect because externally incoherent demands are made in the name of efficiency, accountability, the economy, social peace, and progress.[34] The vulnerable university mediates these incoherent and contradictory demands and they become the day-to-day stressors of academic life.

---

[27]A promise of increasing social mobility that has not been kept not kept; see: Major and Machin (n 22) and Hilary Sommerlad, "The New 'Professionalism' in England and Wales: Talent, Diversity, and a Legal Precariat" in Spencer Headworth and others (eds), *Diversity in Practice: Race, Gender, and Class in Legal and Professional Careers* (Cambridge University Press 2016).

[28]See n 20 on neoliberalism and OECD (n 16): "'It is more important than ever that young people learn the knowledge and skills needed to navigate our unpredictable and changing world,' said OECD Secretary-General Angel Gurría ... Many institutions are evolving to meet changing job market demands". Stefan Collini, *What Are Universities For?* (Penguin 2012).

[29]Marilyn Strathern (ed), *Audit Cultures: Anthropology Studies in Accountability, Ethics and the Academy* (Routledge 2000); Marilyn Strathern, "'Improving Ratings': Audit in the British University System" (1997) 5 European Review 305; Michael Power, *The Audit Society: Rituals of Verification* (Oxford University Press 1999); Stefan Collini, *Speaking of Universities* (Verso 2017). An interesting side effect of the Covid-19 pandemic was the tacit official recognition that research audit *impedes* actual research activity; see: Jack Grove, "UK's Next REF Postponed 'Until Further Notice'" *THE* (24 March 2020) <https://www.timeshighereducation.com/news/uks-next-ref-postponed-until-further-notice> accessed 12 March 2021.

[30]The process is described using the concept of "governance" in Simon Marginson and Mark Considine, *The Enterprise University: Power, Governance and Reinvention in Australia* (Cambridge University Press 2000).

[31]See Alfred D Chandler Jr, *The Visible Hand: The Managerial Revolution in American Business* (Harvard University Press 1977). For a historical analysis of the shift in power within universities over the twentieth and twenty-first centuries, see also: Michael Shattock, "University Governance in Flux. The Impact of External and Internal Pressures on the Distribution of Authority within British Universities: A Synoptic View" (2017) 71 Higher Education Quarterly 384. On managerialism in higher education see: Martin Trow, "Managerialism and the Academic Profession" in Trow (2010) (n 16). Marginson and Considine, *The Enterprise University* (n 30).

[32]Shattock, "University Governance in Flux" (n 31) 391.

[33]For confirmation of the deleterious loss of control see: Anna McKie, "UK Academia 'Increasingly Unsafe' Working Environment" *THE* (9 January 2020) <https://www.timeshighereducation.com/news/uk-academia-increasingly-unsafe-working-environment> accessed 12 March 2021.

[34]See: Graham Ferris, *Uses of Values in Legal Education* (Intersentia 2015) 6.

[35]Liz Morrish, "Pressure Vessels: The Epidemic of Poor Mental Health among Higher Education Staff"(HEPI Occasional Paper 20 2019); Tim O'Brien and Dennis Guiney, "Staff Wellbeing in Higher Education" (Education Support Partnership 2018).

State and market stressors – the private life of the university

The ideological, governmental, regulatory, market, and institutional pressures outlined above have an impact on the lived experience of legal and other academics.[35] These stressors generate a clash of values that itself can serve to undermine academic resilience. The impact is felt by everyone, since vulnerability is universal, but is felt more intensely and with greater damaging effects by those with fewer assets and resilience: the effect of universal vulnerability is therefore particular. The impact can lead to ill health and in some tragic cases, such as that of Malcolm Anderson, death.[36] Institutional responses are often unhelpful because institutions forged in the neoliberal paradigm fail to recognise the deleterious effects of managerialism as a problem.[37] Academics should be able to resist inappropriate pressure and respond as competitive individuals: "We have to look after each other, otherwise we have managers creating a culture where everyone is out for themselves".[38] The undermining of social assets is not seen as a part of the problem, as an analysis informed by assumptions around the liberal subject simply cannot "see" the nature of the problem, even though it is felt and understood at a personal level by very many within higher education.[39] This problem of neoliberal blinkers means we need bridging concepts, such as "resilience" in vulnerability theory.

Another useful bridging set of concepts can be found in regulation of the workplace for safety. In the UK it provides a partial account of how modern academic life degrades resilience through "management standards" that are set out by the UK Health and Safety Executive (HSE).[40] The standards identify six proximate causes of harmful stress in the workplace: "demands" (workload), "control" (autonomy), "support" (resources including collegial culture), "relationships" (avoiding oppressive behaviours by managers), "role" (clarity about what a role entails), and "change" (how well managed and communicated changes are). The standards can be mapped on to sources of resilience in vulnerability theory, specifically: physical ("support"), social ("demands", "support", "relationships", and "role"), ecological ("support"), and existential ("control", "role", and "change"). The HSE approach is helpful because it identifies sources of resilience that lie outside the individual academic and can be used in resistance to harmful work cultures and demands.[41] The standards aid us in envisaging the big picture stressors as they affect individual academics. However, we start our account of the private life of university law schools with an issue not within the purview of the HSE standards, the value conflicts that can arise between academics and managers.[42] Such conflicts are bound up with existential assets in vulnerability theory.

---

[36]Catrin Haf Jones, "Lecturer's Widow Hits Out at Cardiff University Workload" (*BBC News*, 20 February 2020) <www.bbc.co.uk/news/uk-wales-47296631> accessed 31 July 2020.

[37]Thomas Deacon, "Cardiff University Lecturer Hits Out at Insulting 'Suicide Locks' Put on Windows after Tutor's Death" (*Wales Online*, 3 March 2019) <www.walesonline.co.uk/news/wales-news/cardiff-university-lecturer-hits-out-15907286> accessed 31 July 2020.

[38]Anonymous interviewee on the meaning of wellbeing, O'Brien and Guiney, *Staff Wellbeing* (n 35) 7.

[39]Colin James, Caroline Strevens and Rachel Field, "Law Teachers Speak Out: What Do Law Schools Need to Change?" in Michael Legg, Prue Vines and Janet Chan (eds), *The Impact of Technology and Innovation on the Wellbeing of the Legal Profession* (Intersentia 2020) 131.

[40]Health and Safety Executive, *Tackling Work-Related Stress Using The Management Standards Approach: A Step by Step Workbook* (The Stationery Office 2017) <www.hse.gov.uk/pubns/wbk01.pdf> accessed 22 July 2020.

[41]The HSE guidance is closely tied to the enforcement of legal standards upon employers. It is noteworthy how similar the management standards categories are to the categories used by James and others, "Law Teachers Speak Out" (n 39); there is substantial convergence in evidence.

[42]Value conflicts apparently more apparent to academic middle managers than to executive level managers, see: V Lynn Meek and Fiona Q Wood, "Higher Education Governance and Management: Australia" (1998) 11 Higher Education Policy 165, table 2, 173–75. The remit of the HSE would preclude it from commenting upon the rectitude of organisational values or managerial culture.

Legal scholars no longer share consensual understandings of the mission of the discipline or of the educational mission of the university law school.[43] The shift in the UK from an elite higher education system to a mass higher education system left academics unsure of their educational function, as Scott noted in 1995:[44]

> Many universities ... remain committed to a personal engagement between teachers and students, and to individualised (even charismatic) styles of scholarship ... which appear to take little account of either the values or the imperatives of a mass system.

In 2020 fewer university management teams are committed to such "elite" educational ideals, which have been displaced by revenue maximisation, managerial norms, audit compliance, and league table competition.[45] However, many academics remain committed to these educational ideals. Although presented as technocratic and politically neutral these "values or the imperatives of a mass system" are ideologically loaded, and imposing them managerially subjects academics to the reductionism of an ideologically informed neo-liberal system.[46] Hence the importance of challenging the assumptions of unproblematically autonomous academics, universities, and students and reframing our analysis of current pressures through a vulnerability lens.

In addition, the shift from a small relatively culturally homogenous student cohort to a large and more diverse student cohort has affected the university and the law school. A welcome increase in student diversity has aggravated the problems caused by a lack of consensus around the role of and range of values that should inform higher education.[47] In the nineteenth century Newman assumed that all values were knowable and coherently arranged, so that his ideal university simply had to maintain the hierarchy of disciplines.[48] Although Newman's values were restricted in range and unjustifiably static and backwards looking even when he wrote they gained widespread acceptance within academia.[49] Humboldt had a more expansive and forward-looking set of values, yet he also assumed a compatibility of values that would be revealed by the mutually supporting activities of teaching and research.[50] Pluralism, or relativism, denies any such value harmony and holds that there is no rational determinant of best value. Whilst value discourse can identify errors

---

[43] This is not a reiteration of the old tension inherent in professional higher education between liberal (or socio-legal) legal education or preparation for the profession; any consensus over the purpose of higher education that that debate assumes has been lost. Readings, *The University in Ruins* (n 21); R Barnett, *Thinking and Rethinking the University: The Selected Works of Ronald Barnett* (Routledge 2014). The problem is not new, see: Max Weber, *The Vocation Lectures: Science as a Vocation; Politics as a Vocation* (David Owen and Tracy B Strong eds, Rodney Livingstone tr, Hackett Publishing Company 2004) and Chad Wellmon, "The Scholar's Vocation" <https://aeon.co/essays/weber-diagnosed-the-ills-of-the-modern-university-and-prescribed-the-cure> accessed 14 July 2020.

[44] Peter Scott, *The Meanings of Mass Higher Education* (Open University Press 1995) 2.

[45] In the discourse around massification the word "elite" carries different meanings in a rhetorically useful but confusing manner. Elite means small as opposed to large cohorts; elite means preparing the next generation of elite leaders (reproduction of social hierarchy) rather than educating large numbers of skilled knowledge workers; elite means institutions with high prestige and resources; and elite means concerned with the educational flourishing of the students as opposed to serving the economy through the production of human capital. It is the fourth sense of "elite" aspiration that is defended in the text.

[46] See: "State and market stressors – the big picture" above.

[47] For a discussion see: Graham Ferris, *Uses of Values in Legal Education* (Intersentia 2015) ch 1: "The Values of Legal Educators".

[48] John Henry Newman, *The Idea of a University* (Baronius Press Ltd 2006). This book remains an important point of reference in the UK.

[49] Ferris, *Uses of Values* (n 47) 14–25.

[50] Readings, *University in Ruins* (n 21) chs 4 and 5. Weber noted the reality of common disconnection of research and teaching abilities, Weber, *Vocation Lectures* (n 43). The German research university is widely seen as inspiring the modern US research university in the post-bellum nineteenth century.

in argument, ultimately disagreements about the attributes and purposes of a worthwhile life remain that, disagreements.[51] Therefore, earlier consensus within academia around values cannot be taken for granted but requires mobilisation of argument and the seeking of alliances on a case-by-case basis. Today we can no longer assume traditional educational practice in the area of value discourse is sufficient or even justifiable. This raises problems of meaning for legal academics, it threatens their social and existential resilience, and these are vital assets in the context of the modern law school.

The importance of existential assets can be illustrated by reflection upon the reported experiences of academics. Surveys of academics have found that factors associated by the HSE standards with high stress or job dissatisfaction: such as long working hours,[52] work overload ("demands"), and lack of support ("support" and "relationships"), did not prevent academics from reporting satisfaction with their jobs.[53] This is explicable according to self-determination theory: if academics feel intrinsically motivated, competent in the performance of their duties, and part of a community, then we can expect their wellbeing to be supported and their reported job satisfaction to be high.[54] In other words, the existential and social assets of academia can act as a counterweight to relatively discouraging physical assets (hours, relative remuneration, workload). The researcher or researcher teacher are socially recognised types of professional who find meaning in work, people with a worthwhile vocation.[55] Different academics value different aspects of the job differently, some feeling research is the central activity, while others value teaching. However, most academics believe both these activities have inherent value.[56]

The belief in the value of autonomy, research, and teaching explains the decision to become a legal academic and the perseverance and dedication of established academics. Within academia one can find other people who have committed to these values. Therefore, these existential assets also produce social assets, through involvement in formal institutions, such as disciplinary

---

[51] Isaiah Berlin, "The Pursuit of the Ideal" in Isaiah Berlin, *The Proper Study of Mankind: An Anthology of Essays* (Henry Hardy and Roger Hausheer eds, Pimlico 1998).

[52] MY Tytherleigh and others, "Occupational Stress in UK Higher Education Institutions: A Comparative Study of All Staff Categories" (2005) 24 Higher Education Research and Development 41, 50; Chris Chambers and others, "Should You Be Working 100 Hours a Week?" *THE* (20 February 2020); R Fontinha, S Easton and D Van Laar, "Overtime and Quality of Working Life in Academics and Non-Academics: The Role of Perceived Work-Life Balance" (2019) 26 International Journal of Stress Management 173.

[53] Tytherleigh and others, "Occupational Stress" (n 52) 43. See Anthony Bradney, *Conversations, Choices and Chances: The Liberal Law School in the Twenty-First Century* (Hart Publishing 2003) 15–17 <https://www.timeshighereducation.com/features/should-you-be-working-100-hours-week> accessed 12 March 2021. For an alternative contemplation of the issue, see: David Watson, *The Question of Morale: Managing Happiness and Unhappiness in University Life* (Open University Press 2009). For science PhD students, see: Bethan Cornell, "PhD Students and Their Careers" (HEPI Policy Note 25, July 2020) <www.hepi.ac.uk/wp-content/uploads/2020/07/HEPI-Policy-Note-25_PhD-students-careers_FINAL.pdf> accessed 16 July 2020. Identifying three of the HSE stressors listed at text between nn 41 and 42, demands, support, and relationships.

[54] See: Graham Ferris and Rebecca Huxley-Binns, "What Students Care About and Why We Should Care" in Paul Maharg and Caroline Maughan (eds), *Affect and Legal Education: Emotion in Learning and Teaching the Law* (Ashgate 2011) 195; Richard M Ryan and Edward L Deci, *Self-Determination Theory: Basic Psychological Needs in Motivation, Development, and Wellness* (Guilford Press 2017). We can approximately map these aspects of wellbeing noted on to the HSE management standards noted earlier at text between nn 40 and 41: intrinsic motivation ("control", "support", and "change"), competence ("demands", "support", "role", and "change"), being part of a group ("support" and "relationships").

[55] Weber, *Vocation Lectures* (n 43).

[56] For legal scholars in England see: Fiona Cownie, *Legal Academics – Cultures and Identities* (Hart Publishing 2004).

societies,[57] and informal association within the workplace with colleagues. Work inspired by these values is likely to lead to success in one's career, and thus lead to physical assets. Therefore, these existential assets and the relationships and activities they lead to explain why academia remains an attractive place to work for neophytes and established practitioners.[58]

However, assets that reduce vulnerability by providing resilience can also lead to new risks of harm, and this is true of the existential assets incidental to serving the educational goals of research and teaching. This is very clearly shown by a study of zookeepers in the USA which will be used to illuminate the world of legal academics.[59]

Zookeepers feel a strong sense of calling, and this explains why they apply for and serve in jobs that otherwise seem demanding and poorly rewarded in economic terms. Zookeepers value their relationships with the animals in their care and their role in protecting the species from the risks of extinction through breeding programmes. These values feed a sense of calling that provides a source of great satisfaction; it is an existential asset. However, when managers of zoos do not put animal welfare or preservation first then the reaction of many zookeepers is not to leave the job, which no longer is aligned with those values that the zookeeper serves, but to redouble efforts to protect the welfare of the animals and the breeding programmes. The sense of vocation which provides an existential asset also makes zookeepers liable to exploitation – as they will work for free to protect the animals even at the expense of their human and social assets (their health and families and wider social activities).[60]

Legal academics find an analogous meaning in their jobs, through a commitment to research and teaching. Also, they value academic freedom or autonomy in the workplace,[61] both as a thing in itself and as something that permits them to serve the ends of academia. Legal research is very difficult to do without significant freedom, and creative and responsive teaching also requires significant academic freedom. Additionally, some academics believe that they have a responsibility as public intellectuals to challenge abuses of power, in the university, in the justice system, and in society at a national level, and in the global public sphere at an international level.[62] Speaking truth to power requires academic freedom, because power prefers the echo of its own prejudice over truth, and power can be vengeful

---

[57]For legal scholars in England and the UK: Association of Law Teachers, the Socio-Legal Studies Association, Society of Legal Scholars.

[58]Although academia in the UK is significantly less attractive as a career than it was 40 years ago, see: Williams (n 19) 288–89, and Cornell (n 53).

[59]JS Bunderson and JA Thompson, "The Call of the Wild: Zookeepers, Callings, and the Double-Edged Sword of Deeply Meaningful Work" (2009) 54 Administrative Science Quarterly 32. For academics see: Fontinha and others, "Overtime" (n 52).

[60]Bunderson and Thompson, "The Call of the Wild" (n 59).

[61]Control being the HSE concept closest to autonomy, and which is constructed by institutional forces, and threatened by changes in the institutional structure of higher education taking place over the last 40 years and discussed above.

[62]Robert E Calvert (ed), *To Restore American Democracy: Political Education and the Modern University* (Rowman & Littlefield Publishers 2006); Bruce LR Smith, Jeremy D Meyer and A Lee Fritschler, *Closed Minds? Politics and Ideology in American Universities* (Brookings Institution Press 2008).

[63]John Ross, "University Staff Must Find Their Voice, Says Murdoch Whistleblower" *THE* (London, 1 July 2020) <https://www.timeshighereducation.com/news/university-staff-must-find-their-voice-says-murdoch-whistleblower> accessed 12 March 2021; Philip Moriarty, "Sorry, Marketers, But I Am Not Your Brand" *THE* (6 July 2020) <https://www.timeshighereducation.com/opinion/sorry-marketers-iam-not-your-brand> accessed 12 March 2021; Scholars at Risk, *Free to Think 2019: Report of the Scholars at Risk Academic Freedom Monitoring Project* <www.scholarsatrisk.org/resources/free-to-think-2019/> accessed 14 July 2020; Richard Watermeyer, *Competitive Accountability in Academic Life: The Struggle of Social Impact and Public Legitimacy* (Edward Elgar

if discomforted.[63] Therefore, there is serious reason to believe that freedom in the conduct of work is an integral part of the existential asset that sustains academic commitment.

Indeed, there is reason to believe that modern business organisations seek to encourage employees to share an intrinsic sense of devotion to institutional ends. The artist and the academic have become the model for people so motivated by the ideals of their activity they will drive themselves if free to conduct their work.[64] Academics constantly self-educate, develop new understanding, skills, and techniques in an intrinsically motivated drive to excel in those activities they value.[65] Thus, it seems the shared purpose of the university and the academic, as well as the wider society, should lead to a mutually beneficial relationship. Established legal academics can continue to develop and the universities can encourage such mutual benefits by lifting insecurity from new academics, enabling them to devote themselves to the collective aims of the institution. Unfortunately, the neoliberal law school is subject to those institutional structures, which militate against this harmonious outcome.

Educational values in teaching and research are in extreme tension with neoliberal values. The image of the student as a consumer of a service industry distorts the educational relationship which is inevitably unequal and therefore ill-suited to an arm's-length contractual analysis.[66] I have critiqued this consumer ideology elsewhere:[67] it fails to acknowledge the positional aspect of education,[68] it cannot cope with the transformative aspects of education,[69] and it is only justifiable in the context of a stable world which renders it unsuitable for our world.[70] For a teaching academic this value conflict is manifest in multiple irritations: pressure to seek "student satisfaction" (embedded in use of student surveys in staff performance appraisals) rather than student growth, attempts to enforce a corporate image in communications with potential and actual students which is seen as an aspect of marketing,[71] and generally a shift from an ideal of education as a caring relationship to one of education as a regulated market relationship.[72] The day-to-day impacts of the tension between educational values and a market in educational services are facilitated by audit culture and managerialism.

Research priorities can be distorted by a view of the purpose of research as a successful search for funding,[73] and the cultivation of proxies for impact can impede research inspired by a concern to effect lasting real-world change as well as research

---

2020) 40 (Robert Buckingham); Joyce Lau, "University of Hong Kong Fires Occupy Central Founder Benny Tai" *THE* (28 July 2020) <https://www.timeshighereducation.com/news/university-hong-kong-fires-occupy-central-founder-benny-tai> accessed 12 March 2021.

[64]Andrew Ross, *Low Pay, High Profile: The Global Push for Fair Labor* (The New Press 2004) ch 7: "The Mental Labor Problem".

[65]An impulse that can become problematic in the modern university, see: Watermeyer, *Competitive Accountability* (n 63).

[66]It is an example of an inevitable inequality: Martha Albertson Fineman, "Vulnerability and Inevitable Inequality" (n 12).

[67]Ferris, *Uses of Values* (n 47) 44–56.

[68]David F Laboree, *Someone Has to Fail: The Zero-Sum Game of Public Schooling* (Harvard University Press 2010).

[69]Peter Jarvis, *Teaching, Learning and Education in Late Modernity: The Selected Works of Peter Jarvis* (Routledge 2012). Student transformation violates the axioms of rationality embodied by economic man.

[70]Douglass C North (n 14) ch 3.

[71]John Ross, "University staff must find their voice, says Murdoch whistleblower" *THE* (London, 1 July 2020) <https://www.timeshighereducation.com/news/university-staff-must-find-their-voice-says-murdoch-whistle blower> accessed 12 March 2021; Philip Moriarty, "Sorry, Marketers, But I Am Not Your Brand" *THE* (6 July 2020) <https://www.timeshighereducation.com/opinion/sorry-marketers-iam-not-your-brand> accessed 12 March 2021.

[72]Nel Noddings, *Caring: A Feminine Approach to Ethics and Moral Education* (University of California Press 2013).

[73]Thornton, *Privatising the Public University* (n 20) ch 5.

seeking understanding and critiquing.[74] The shift from research based on curiosity and academic values to research undertaken to meet performance targets can erode researcher identity and motivation and undermine the quality of research.[75]

Linked to the reconceptualisation of the learner as a buyer of education is the individual as the embodiment of human capital. There is some overlap between the idea of human capital (education, work experience, skills) and human assets in vulnerability theory. In the internal life of UK education, and across many higher education systems internationally, human capital theory is embedded in the concept of employability.[76] In so far as employability is directed to developing the capabilities of students there has been a willingness to integrate it into the legal curriculum.[77] However, the rhetoric of employability can deceive students as to the relationship between educational goals and curriculum content and employment opportunities.[78] Human capital theory and employability do not recognise the large role played by cultural capital and institutional reputation in professional recruitment, projecting instead a strongly functional and "meritocratic" labour market.[79]

Thus, the impact of employability on teaching academics is varied. At its most positive, it justifies the teaching and accessing of soft skills and the use of clinical legal education. When combined with law school recruitment of students to maximise income from tuition, it puts pressure on the honesty of the legal educational project, given the realities for many students of the professional job market.[80] Finally, when used to argue for an impoverished curriculum emphasising adaptation of the student to the market or, even worse, to what the student imagines the market to demand, it risks reducing the purpose of higher education,

---

[74]Watermeyer, *Competitive Accountability* (n 63). Cornell (n 53). Shift Learning, "What Researchers Think About the Research Culture They Work In" (Welcome 2020) <https://wellcome.ac.uk/reports/what-researchers-think-about-research-culture> accessed 22 July 2020. M Joan Wilson and WR Sexson, "The Positive and Negative Roles of Grant Funding as Mechanisms for Societal Transformation and the Development of Community Resilience" (2021) The Law Teacher (this issue).

[75]Hine Jane Waitere and others, "Choosing Whether to Resist or Reinforce the New Managerialism: The Impact of Performance-Based Research Funding on Academic Identity" (2011) 30 Higher Education Research & Development 205. Shift Learning, "What Researchers Think" (n 74).

[76]Although the concept is contested, reflecting in part the educational and the human capital approaches taken to employability. Phillip Brown, Anthony Hesketh and Sara Wiliams, "Employability in a Knowledge-driven Economy" (2003) 16 Journal of Education and Work 107, 110 point out that some definitions of employability imply human capital formation can somehow generate job market opportunities, eg: "employability is about having the capability to gain initial employment, maintain employment and obtain new employment if required". Contrast with: "In essence, the emphasis is on developing critical, reflective abilities, with a view to empowering and enhancing the learner. Employment is a by-product of this enabling process." Lee Harvey, "Transitions from Higher Education to Work" (Briefing paper, 2003) <www.qualityresearchinternational.com/esecttools/esectpubs/harveytransitions.pdf> accessed 21 July 2020.

[77]David Rigg, "Embedding Employability in Assessment: Searching for the Balance between Academic Learning and Skills Development in Law: A Case Study" (2013) 47 The Law Teacher 404; Jenny Knox and Melanie Stone, "Embedding Employability Skills for the Legal Professionals of the Future" (2019) 53 The Law Teacher 90; Simon Brooman and Sarah Stirk, "Who Am I? Using Reflective Practice and Self-determination to Redefine 'Employability' in Legal Education" (2020) 41 Liverpool Law Review 79; and in an Australian context: Francina Cantatore, "Boosting Law Graduate Employability: Using a Pro Bono Teaching Clinic to Facilitate Experiential Learning in Commercial Law Subjects" (2015) 25 Legal Education Review 147.

[78]Penny Childs, Nigel Firth and Hugo de Rijke, "The Gap between Law Student Career Aspirations and Employment Opportunities" (2014) 48 The Law Teacher 51; Julian Webb and others, "Setting Standards: The Future of Legal Services Education and Training Regulation in England and Wales" (Legal Education and Training Review 2013) 2.132–2.143.

[79]See: sources at n 23 and Lisa Webley and others, "Access to a Career in the Legal Profession in England and Wales: Race, Class and the Role of Educational Background" and Hilary Sommerlad, "The New 'Professionalism' in England and Wales: Talent, Diversity, and a Legal Precariat" in Spencer Headworth and others (eds), *Diversity in Practice: Race, Gender, and Class in Legal and Professional Careers* (Cambridge University Press 2016).

[80]Graeme Broadbent and Pamela Sellman, "Great Expectations? Law Schools, Websites and 'the Student Experience'" (2013) 47 The Law Teacher 44.

similar to the way the idea of the student as consumer does. It is shaped by an ideology of the student as an entity that seeks to invest in the self as an asset which is being shaped into something that will serve the market. It instrumentalises the self. This market orientation can be alienating for academics who view legal education as equipping students to serve democracy or justice rather than only serving private economic values.

Audit has an impact upon the academic at innumerable points. It can be mischievous in several ways. It typically adds to workload and can undermine academic feelings of "control". It can generate "role" conflicts, as it imposes administrative tasks upon either academic staff or administrative staff, and when this role uncertainty is resolved by adding tasks to the academic role there is a failure of that "support" for academics that should be supplied by professional services within the university. Further, the reasons for audit-motivated change are often introduced through a rhetoric of teaching quality or competitive excellence that obfuscates the purpose of changes and thereby again undermines "control" and "change". Audit is one of those points, noted above, at which a clash of values informing teaching and research practice manifests in the degradation of resilience.

The Research Excellence Framework (REF) is the current iteration of research audit in the UK.[81] The Stern Review, the tone of which is more cheerleader for REF than critical, noted that the REF 2014 had been expensive, tended to distort research and set up disincentives to undertake long-term or fundamental research, had negative effects on the development and careers of some academics, had discriminatory impact on women, ethnic minority or overseas researchers and disabled researchers, and may have had a negative impact on interdisciplinary research.[82] Watermeyer has explored the perverse effects of "impact" in the REF at length: amongst the negative effects are damaged relationships with research subjects and potential users of research, hyperbolic and unsubstantiated claims, institutional focus on claimable impact rather than actual impact, and reward of narrative plausibility over reality.[83] If we turn to the review of the evidence submitted to Lord Stern for his review, we find that academics subjected to REF found it increased "demands" (workload) on their time which led to working excessive hours. The process also had a negative impact on their sense of "control", and was perceived as having potentially career-destroying consequences. It seems to have been disproportionately damaging to young researchers and women.[84]

Audit of teaching is less well established in the UK. It affects academics primarily through internal institutional learning and teaching bureaucracies. Audit of teaching and learning does not actually examine teaching and learning that takes place within law schools: the model is not the inspection but the regulatory audit. Regulatory audit "audits" the mechanisms of internal audit; it is a type of self-regulation (internal audit) that is subject to external monitoring (external audit).[85] The consequences are a

---

[81] Lord Nicholas Stern, *Building on Success and Learning from Experience: An Independent Review of the Research Excellence Framework* [10] <https://assets.publishing.service.gov.uk/government/uploads/system/uploads/attachment_data/file/541338/ind-16-9-ref-stern-review.pdf> accessed 22 July 2020, notes the pioneering nature of UK research audit with the first iteration known as the Research Selectivity Exercise (RSE).

[82] Stern (n 81) [23]–[48].

[83] Watermeyer, *Competitive Accountability* (n 63). M Joan Wilson and WR Sexson, "The Positive and Negative Roles of Grant Funding as Mechanisms for Societal Transformation and the Development of Community Resilience" (2021) The Law Teacher (this issue).

[84] Erik Arnold and others, "Review of the Research Excellence Framework: Evidence Report" (Technopolis Group 2018) <https://assets.publishing.service.gov.uk/government/uploads/system/uploads/attachment_data/file/768162/research-excellence-framework-review-evidence-report.pdf> accessed 22 July 2020. Grove, *THE* (n 29) shows the government is aware that REF actually impedes research.

[85] Matt O'Leary, Vanessa Cui and Amanda French, *Understanding, Recognising and Rewarding Teaching Quality in Higher Education: An Exploration of the Impact and Implications of the Teaching Excellence Framework* (UCU

proliferation of administrative tasks, a tendency to restrict delivery and assessment to recognised pro forma types, and a managerial emphasis on the production of records for audit. These processes affect "demands" (through task proliferation), "control" (through bureaucratic homogenisation), "support" (as the production of audit records and compliance with "quality" requirements tend to fall on academics), "role" (as many of the requirements are administrative) and "change" (as the ever-changing requirements are imposed in a non-negotiable manner as a requirement of quality).

Both research and teaching audits are imposed through a performance management system which ties audit to managerialism in general and new public management in particular. Performativity demands that tasks not only be done but be demonstrably done. "Performance" is then tied to advancement or disciplinary sanction. In this way, performance is set up as a competitive system, with academics vying to out-perform each other in order to obtain success. This audit culture intervention results in a loss of "control" (as what constitutes performance is within managerial discretion), loss of "support" (as it puts a strain on collegiality), impairment of "relationships" (as managers become judges of performance rather than facilitators of colleagues' development), and leads to a constant tension in "roles" (as managers and managed renegotiate "SMART" performance objectives annually). Finally, disagreements about values are enacted through the obfuscating language and practices of performance management.

In short it is apparent that the big picture stressors identified above are facilitated by institutional managerial processes applied to academics. Academics find their resilience undermined by their institutions in ways that we can map on to HSE standards or vulnerability theory. In the realm of value disagreements, in the way this operates requires us to use vulnerability theory alone. Vulnerability theory, self-determination theory, and HSE standards are all congruent with an emphasis on the need for workplace "control" of responsibilities by academics, greater "support" in the face of rising "demands", greater clarity around "role", more negotiation around "changes" being introduced, and the importance of supportive relationships in the workplace. Vulnerability theory and self-determination theory agree on the importance of the internal motivation and constructed autonomy of the academic worker. Vulnerability theory identifies the vital role played by the self-identity and sense of meaning derived by academics from their work and as is elaborated below on the need for academics to look beyond the university management structures to the collegial mutual support, the legal discipline, and the union where unions exist.

How does the "invulnerable" academic respond to existential discordance?

Trow argued that:[86]

> Almost everything in a university depends on the inner motivations of teachers – their sense of pride, their intellectual involvement with their subjects, their professional commitments to the role of teacher, their love of students or of learning – these and others are among the forces that lead teachers to bring their full resources to the teaching relationships. And these motivations of academics are usually quite independent of unpredictable external assessments, and the remote incentives and punishments that can be attached to them.

2019). Power (n 29) explains how this is normal in regulation through audit, first the audited activity must make itself capable of audit, then government audit is usually of internal processes of audit.

[86]Martin Trow, "Managerialism and the Academic Profession" in Trow (2010) (n 16) 283.

We have argued this finding of meaning in the academic role is an existential asset that provides a sense of meaning and can be called a sense of vocation. In this section we explore the difficulties posed by the big picture stressors mediated through university and law school managerialism to an academic with a sense of vocation.

Vulnerability theory tells us we must look to the institutional forces that are either supporting or degrading our resilience, and that we are likely to need social assets if we are to thrive. However, the default assumption of our neoliberal world is that we should seek to overcome any difficulties independently. The liberal subject is an autonomous being and does not need support. However, she is faced with a dilemma, put to a choice between vocational values and managerial values in the modern law school and university. In thinking about this dilemma, we should bear in mind the analogous dilemma facing zookeepers explored above.

The scholars and support staff within universities risk being caught between two equally dispiriting alternatives: give up on the idealised identity of the scholar, educator, and member of the discipline and seek to serve the powers that be, the route of the apparatchik; or, sacrifice oneself in service of the ideals of scholarship and discipline and ameliorate the damage done by ignorant managers in order to serve the true purposes of the university, the route of the zookeeper. The route of the apparatchik sacrifices existential assets in the service of physical and social assets, the route of the zookeeper subordinates all other types of asset to the cause of the existential asset.

Working within a law school that is recruiting as many students as possible whilst gaming research to maximise REF results, and also systematically under-resourcing teaching, and using performance management to enact its institutional priorities, creates a dilemma for individual legal academics: become an apparatchik or a zookeeper?

Other factors exacerbate this dilemma. Academically weaker students require more teaching attention and time to develop than academically strong students, but market logic is directly contrary to the educational logic. In the UK the ability to pay is supported by government loans for home students and has become more important in decisions on admission as the diversity of applicants expands.[87] This may be a welcome outcome in principle, but to respond to it in an educationally sound manner requires considerable development of teaching materials and ideally more customised teaching to individuals or groups. However, such methods have cost implications that militate against their deployment institutionally, putting pressure on academics to absorb the costs by working longer hours, or more intensively, or both. Diversity among entering students should compel diverse progress and time commitment options, but the costs and administrative challenges of ever-rising numbers push towards ever greater emphasis on getting students through as quickly as possible.

To go down the apparatchik route is to risk alienation in the job, as well as a loss of existential assets. To go down the zookeeper route risks overwork, exhaustion, and a loss of human and social assets. It is hard to see alternatives to this dilemma for the academic deemed to be autonomous, independent, and self-sufficient, an academic bound to be committed to competitive excellence. If we instead accept that such a

[87] See: *Patterns and Trends in UK Higher Education 2018* (Universities UK 2018) <www.universitiesuk.ac.uk/facts-and-stats/data-and-analysis/Documents/patterns-and-trends-in-uk-higher-education-2018.pdf> accessed 30 July 2020. Older students are a decreasing part of the student body, as are part-time students, and deprived areas are underrepresented.

being and such values are not only unattainable but undesirable, and recognise vulnerability, it opens up possibilities and an exciting, productive way forward.

How does the vulnerable academic respond to existential discordance?

The reader of this article is likely to be an academic working in a law school, university, or college. Although some of what follows is specific to the UK, the basic principles are drawn from vulnerability theory and should be applicable *mutatis mutandis* in other jurisdictions.

Discussion at the workshop turned to what could be done to counteract developments, pervasive across institutions and jurisdictions, that are damaging to educational purposes of learning and research and degrading of sources of resilience for academics. We might start with the approach to analogous problems within schools taken by Sir Ken Robinson:[88]

> You can be part of the change. To do that, you need three forms of understanding: a *critique* of the way things are, a *vision* of how they should be, and a *theory of change* for how to move from one to the other.

Vulnerability theory can provide us with a general theoretical approach to critique and vision, and through its applications some guidance on a theory of change. We also need to remember that academics have power and that the law school is typical of educational institutions in being complex and unstable:[89]

> It [the educational system] is neither monolithic nor unchanging, which is why you can do something about it. It has many faces, many intersecting interests, and many potential points of innovation.

Finally, we need to be aware of the need to seek change at various levels, because power structures operate at various levels:[90]

> If you're involved in education in any way you have three options: you can make changes within the system, you can press for changes to the system, or you can take initiatives outside the system.

At the workshop there was some perception that these three levels or options were contradictory. However, upon reflection I think they can be seen as complementary. We can develop our research and teaching whilst opposing damaging and degrading features of managerialism and working for a fairer and more humane ideology in our societies. What enables us to do this is not serendipity but vulnerability theory's availability as a guide on how to act coherently across different levels of action.

This article has attempted to establish links between some of these different levels and potential means of action in its analysis. A sense of vocation is an existential asset that should not be lightly relinquished. However, we are not able to withstand a loss of too many of our other sources of resilience in its defence. We are vulnerable and need to look to other sources of resilience. One reason for the use of HSE standards above was that they are a resource that can be used in negotiating with managerial power in the UK. The state has bounded the power of managers through Health and Safety legislation and placed duties upon employers to safeguard the mental and physical health of employees. Violations of

---

[88]Ken Robinson and Lou Aronica, *Creative Schools: Revolutionizing Education from the Ground Up* (Penguin 2016) 133, italics in the original.
[89]ibid 138.
[90]ibid 154.

the standards can lead to legal liability if employee health is impaired. We should look to the law which can counterbalance private power and act as a source of resilience.

There is a recognition within academia that wellbeing needs to be protected and enhanced. Although many institutional initiatives portray resilience as an individual capacity, rather than an institutionally supported capacity, there is agreement on the value of supporting resilience. One reason to incorporate self-determination approaches with vulnerability theory is to emphasise the potential for action within institutions that show responsiveness to the needs of people. The ideas of "resilience" and of human needs taken from self-determination theory are bridging concepts to vulnerability theory. Using bridging concepts enables people to argue for responsive law schools and pushing institutions to go beyond individualised programmes of skills or counselling for academics.

Not all changes we have reviewed are wholly negative. As we saw with employability there is room for creative engagement with some neoliberal initiatives. However, it is important to keep a theoretically informed critical eye and to reject the underlying assumptions contained in some versions of employability. It may be possible to align demands with educational values, but whenever there is discordance it is important to align the external demand to educational values and not vice versa. The workshop was held with the support of educational and disciplinary institutions and hopefully the outputs in this special issue will strengthen authors' careers. Yet the workshop's participants were clearly critical of many features of the contemporary law school and were reaching towards ways and means to oppose them and reassert academic values in our practice.

Educational systems and educational institutions leave significant space for academic freedom of action for the reasons pointed out by Trow in the quotation on the inner motivations of teachers above.[91] Although it is the record of research or teaching and learning that is managed so aggressively, ultimately everyone knows it is the actual research and teaching and learning that will sustain the law school as an educational endeavour and as an economic entity. This protects individual and collegial freedom and opens up routes for negotiation of the practices of the law school with managers.

Through our disciplinary and professional organisations, we have routes for collective responses to institutional and governmental arguments and actions. One noticeable feature of neoliberal managerial action is to try to reduce the influence of disciplinary organisation upon teaching and research in the university.[92] However, given that the disciplines are constitutive of the knowledge and skills that the university supplies and such a function is what justifies the university, there are limits to this disempowering ploy. Law schools have recognised for a long time the potential for professional standards to be used in institutional struggles over resource allocation.[93] Both disciplinary and professional organisations offer assets to legal academics engaged in resistance to anti-educational institutional pressures.

Academics in the UK can join University and College Unions, engage in collective bargaining, and push for the effective involvement of the academic staff in the governance of the university. In the USA surviving traditions of faculty governance can be used,[94]

[91] Robinson makes a similar point; ibid 152.

[92] Martin Trow, "The American Academic Department as a Context for Learning" (1976) 1 Studies in Higher Education 11; Marginson and Considine, *The Enterprise University* (n 30) 10, 164–74; Thornton, *Privatising the Public University* (n 20) 115–23.

[93] Brian Z Tamanaha, *Failing Law Schools* (University of Chicago Press 2012) ch 2.

[94] Ellen Schrecker, *The Lost Soul of Higher Education: Corporatization, the Assault on Academic Freedom, and the End of the American University* (The New Press 2010).

even though a key factor undermining both faculty governance and union activity is the large number of staff on precarious (non-faculty) contracts.

Finally, vulnerability theory represents an attempt to displace the liberal subject. Society, the economy, and the educational system respond to the stories we tell ourselves about ourselves. The story told by vulnerability theory is more realistic and responsive to the human condition than the story told by neoliberal theory. Asserting and reflecting upon this truth is itself an act of resistance and a source of resilience for our colleagues and ourselves.

Disclosure Statement

No potential conflict of interest was reported by the author.

OPEN ACCESS

Rethinking the neoliberal university: embracing vulnerability in English law schools?

Doug Morrison and Jessica Guth

ABSTRACT

This paper draws on our continuing work on the neoliberal and marketised law school and seeks to understand how we might apply vulnerability theory to address some of the problems resulting from current higher education and law school contexts. After outlining our understanding of vulnerability theory and summarising what we believe are some of the ills of a neoliberal law school, this paper argues that vulnerability theory allows us to reframe our thinking about academic labour and law schools on a theoretical level. As such it is useful for a longer-term project which seeks to challenge existing structures. For more immediate concerns however, the paper suggests, vulnerability theory is less useful because it does not yet provide tools which can be easily operationalised to make a significant difference in our everyday academic lives.

Introduction

Before commencing it needs to be clear that it is beyond the scope of this paper to analyse or even highlight the increasing literature around the marketisation of universities globally. However, what we will argue is that many of the problems universities currently face can be and are linked to the impact of this marketisation process, which in turn is driven by the influence of neoliberalism. In our analysis our focus will inevitably fall upon university law schools and in turn the legal sector, which is where our lived experience is based. In doing so we accept that this analysis captures the debate at a micro rather than the macro level and as such does not seek to address the wider socio-economic and political issues raised by the impact and influence of neoliberalism. Caveats aside, we submit that higher education (HE) in England and Wales and perhaps the world overall is broken.[1] Universities are in (financial) trouble, academics and students are in the middle of a mental health crisis, exacerbated by Covid-19, workloads are unsustainable and students are pitched against each other in an ever more competitive

[1]See Frank Furedi, *Wasted: Why Education Isn't Educating* (Continuum 2009); Henry A Giroux, *Neoliberalism's War on Higher Education* (Haymarket Books 2014); Stefan Collini, *Speaking of Universities* (Verso 2017); Bryan Alexander, *Academia Next: The Futures of Higher Education* (John Hopkins University Press 2020). Importantly, such views are not limited to academic publications, and resonate at least anecdotally, with the lived experiences of those involved in higher education, for example social media comments on Twitter, stories published in the *Times Higher* or on platforms such as WonkHE. Moreover literature focused on the UK and US provides further insight into some of the issues raised by these stories even where they also point to strengths and possible solutions.

environment.[2] Law schools exemplify and perhaps even amplify the ills of the marketised neoliberal university[3] linked inextricably to a changing (legal services) labour market kept afloat by increasing numbers of (paralegal) workers carrying out mostly routine tasks and offering little job satisfaction or financial reward.[4] In the UK research with the legal professions,[5] students[6] and to some extent also academics[7] paints a bleak picture pointing to mental health and wellbeing as an important issue that needs to be addressed urgently. Research from other jurisdictions, Australia and the US tells a similar story.[8] In parallel, literature on the neoliberal university,[9] the marketisation of education[10] and changes in the legal services sector[11] can help us explain some of the reasons why things are at this apparent breaking point.

However, understanding the context in which we find ourselves and even understanding how we got here merely provides the foundations for us to think constructively about how we might make things better, how we might reconceptualise HE generally and legal education specifically. This paper seeks to explore vulnerability theory as one specific example of how we can seek to think differently about our roles as legal academics within law schools and broader institutions. It questions the extent to which vulnerability theory can help us in a reframing of academic work that focuses our minds on collegiality, collaboration and support, and on our mutual dependencies and consider the evolving structures that shape them and therefore might help us produce more meaningful research, scholarship and teaching. We consider how we might embrace these ideas on a theoretical and a practical level and argue that vulnerability theory is theoretically interesting but practically problematic.[12]

---

[2]Mike Molesworth, Richard Scullion and Elizabeth Nixon (eds), *The Marketisation of Higher Education and the Student as a Consumer* (Routledge 2011).

[3]Margaret Thornton, *Privatising the Public University: The Case of Law* (Routledge 2012); Brian Z Tamanaha, *Failing Law Schools* (University of Chicago Press 2012).

[4]Andrew Francis, *At the Edge of Law* (Ashgate 2011); Richard Susskind, *Tomorrow's Lawyers* (2nd edn, OUP 2017); Jessica Guth and Kathryn Dutton, "SQE-ezed Out: SRA, Status and Stasis" (2018) 52 The Law Teacher 425; Hilary Sommerlad and others, "England and Wales: A Legal Profession in the Vanguard of Professional Transformation?" in Richard L Abel and others (eds), *Lawyers in 21st-Century Societies Vol 1: National Reports* (Hart Publishing 2020).

[5]Richard Collier, "'Love Law, Love Life': Neoliberalism, Wellbeing and Gender in the Legal Profession – The Case of Law School" (2014) 17 Legal Ethics 202; Richard Collier, "Wellbeing in the Legal Profession: Reflections on Recent Developments (or, What Do We Talk About When We Talk About Wellbeing?)" (2016) 23 International Journal of the Legal Profession 41; Emma Jones, Rajvinder Samra and Mathijs Lucassen, "The World at Their Fingertips? The Mental Wellbeing of Online Distance-Based Law Students" (2019) 53 The Law Teacher 49.

[6]Caroline Strevens and Clare Wilson, "Law Student Wellbeing in the UK: A Call for Curriculum Intervention" (2016) 11(1) Journal of Commonwealth Law and Legal Education 44; Lydia Bleasdale and Sarah Humphreys, "Undergraduate Resilience Research Project" (Leeds Institute for Teaching Excellence 2018) <https://teachingexcellence.leeds.ac.uk/wp-content/uploads/sites/89/2018/01/LITEbleasdalehumphreys_fullreport_online.pdf> accessed 26 May 2020.

[7]J Clare Wilson and Caroline Strevens, "Perceptions of Psychological Well-being in UK Law Academics" (2018) 42 The Law Teacher 335.

[8]Rachel Field, James Duffy and Colin James (eds), *Promoting Law Student and Lawyer Well-Being in Australia and Beyond* (Routledge 2016); Kathryne M Young, *How to Be Sort of Happy in Law School* (Stanford University Press 2018).

[9]See for example Giroux (n 1); Dorothy Bottrell and Catherine Manathunga (eds), *Resisting Neoliberalism in Higher Education Volume 1* (Palgrave 2019); Catherine Manathunga and Dorothy Bottrell (eds), *Resisting Neoliberalism in Higher Education Volume 2* (Palgrave 2019).

[10]See for example David Palfreyman and Ted Tapper, *Reshaping the University: The Rise of the Regulated Market in Higher Education* (Oxford University Press 2014); David Palfreyman and Ted Tapper, "The Marketization of English Higher Education and the Financing of Tuition Fees" (2016) 14(1) London Review of Education 47.

[11]See for example Susskind (n 4); Francis (n 4); Catherine Shephard, "Strategies for Managing Change and the Use of Paraprofessionals: A Cross-Sector Study for the Benefit of post-LETR Providers of Legal Services. Part Two: The Legal Services Sector and the Shared Management Agenda" (2016) 67 Northern Ireland Legal Quarterly 241.

[12]The authors are aware that other theoretical frameworks exist and could be used to address some, or perhaps all, of the issues we raise. However, this paper fits within a special issue the focus of which is vulnerability theory. As such our approach is to examine and evaluate the role of vulnerability theory in addressing the ills, as we see them, of the neoliberal university.

We begin by outlining our understanding and interpretation of vulnerability theory and how we have thought about it in the context of academic work and the organisation of labour.[13] We then sketch some of the issues raised by marketised, neoliberal universities and law schools as we see and experience them, before considering how thinking about vulnerability and resilience can help reframe some of the issues shaping our academic lives.

Vulnerability theory and academic work

Vulnerability theory offers an attractive framework in which to think about contexts which appear to be causing us harm. Fineman notes that

> Vulnerability theory provides a template with which to refocus critical attention, raising new questions and challenging established assumptions about individual and state responsibility and the role of law, as well as allowing us to address social relationships of inevitable inequality.[14]

As well as thinking about state level responsibility to set up and regulate systems such as healthcare systems, financial systems and education systems in ways which take account of our vulnerability as human beings, we argue that the theory can also prove useful in contexts which are not directly about state responsibility per se but about the responsibility of organisations which have control and responsibility towards us as human beings in general or in specific areas of our lives.[15]

Fineman further suggests;

> A vulnerability approach argues that the state must be responsive to the realities of human vulnerability and its corollary, social dependency, as well as to situations reflecting inherent or necessary inequality, when it initially establishes or sets up mechanisms to monitor these relationships and institutions.[16]

This can easily and almost seamlessly be applied to our context in which the university (taken to mean individual institutions as well as the sector overall depending on context) must be responsive to the vulnerabilities of its academics (and other staff and of course students) as well as the relationships, interdependencies and power structures within which we all work. Universities must do this, we argue, in terms of their formal structures and mechanisms, policies and procedures or what we might call their public life, as well as through their culture, values and behaviours in what we might be termed the private life of universities.

Because "social problems need social or collective, not just individual, solutions"[17] a key effort in utilising vulnerability theory to help address the ills of a neoliberal university must be focused on collegiality and support of each other, paying particular attention to how the formal structures shape these interactions and either support or hinder positive interdependencies and how individuals within law schools experience

---

[13]This section is necessarily brief and should be read in the context of this special issue as a whole through which vulnerability theory is discussed in much greater detail.

[14]Martha Albertson Fineman, "Vulnerability and Inevitable Inequality" (2017) 4 Oslo Law Review 133, 134.

[15]See in general Sean Coyle, "Vulnerability and the Liberal Order" in Martha Albertson Fineman and Anna Grear, *Vulnerability: Reflections on a New Ethical Foundation for Law and Politics* (Ashgate 2013).

[16]Fineman, "Vulnerability and Inevitable Inequality" (n 14) 134.

[17]Fineman, "Vulnerability and Inevitable Inequality" (n 14) 141.

the interactions. This is important, because it serves to remind us that vulnerability is not only organisational, but situational and as such is "an embodied experience and not exclusively a structural one".[18] For us then, vulnerability theory offers a different way of thinking about universities and in particular university law schools, the work carried out within them and the impact that university structures, workloads and culture have. It allows us to shift our focus away from discourse about autonomy and individual responsibility and on to relationships, structures and social responsibility. It allows us to think of university law schools not simply as a collection of (competing) individuals but as institutions built on relationships and interdependencies. This organic rather than solely structural view reminds us not only of our interdependencies and shared goals, but also of our shared resilience.[19] It is the latter realisation that, we argue, might prove a useful first step to reframing the neoliberal university for long enough to allow us to think creatively about alternative approaches to the organisation of academic labour which are less harmful to those inhabiting the academic space.

The neoliberal law school: what's wrong with academia?

Having set out our interpretation of vulnerability theory in the previous section, we now turn our attention to the neoliberal law school in order to outline briefly some of the issues which we think vulnerability theory must help address. In order to do so we draw briefly on the work of others as a means of identifying common themes, different conceptualisations vis-à-vis the issues, as well as a means of demonstrating that ideas as well as terms are, to some extent at least, contested.[20]

As indicated earlier, many of the problems universities face can be linked to the intensification of the neoliberal agenda. As Giroux suggests,

> Four decades of neoliberal policies have resulted in an economic Darwinism that promotes privatization, commodification, free trade, and deregulation. It privileges personal responsibility over larger social forces, reinforces the gap between the rich and the poor ... it fosters a mode of public pedagogy that privileges the entrepreneurial subject while encouraging a value system that promotes self-interest, if not unchecked selfishness.[21]

For education this means,

> ... high stakes testing, skill-based teaching, traditional curriculum, and memorization drills. Ideologically, the pedagogical emphasis is the antithesis of a critical approach to teaching and learning, emphasizing a pedagogy of conformity, and a curriculum marked by vulgar "vocationalist instrumentality".[22]

And, though writing in the US context, Giroux also captures much of what is happening to HE across many western countries including the UK,

---

[18]Coyle (n 15) 70.

[19]Martha Albertson Fineman, "Vulnerability and Social Justice" (2019) 53 Valparasio University Law Review 341, 357 at 368.

[20]See for example Taylor C Boas and Jordan Gans-Morse, "Neoliberalism: From New Liberal Philosophy to Anti-Liberal Slogan" (2009) 44 St Comp Int 137; the various contributions by Bottrell and Manathunga (n 9). Many of the pieces cited, while outlining the problems, also point to the strengths and continuing reputation of Western HE as well as the resistance to neoliberal ideas. This is of course true and important but does not take away from the day-to-day experience on which these points are based.

[21]Giroux (n 1) 1.

[22]Giroux (n 1) 29, citing Graeme Turner, *What's Become of Cultural Studies* (Sage 2011) 183; Henry A Giroux, *Education and the Crisis of Public Values*(Paradigm Publishers 2012).

> Universities are being defunded, tuition fees are skyrocketing, faculty salaries are shrinking as workloads are increasing, and faculty are being reduced to a subaltern class of migrant laborers. Corporate management schemes are being put in place underpinned by market-like principles, based on metrics, control, and display of performance. The latter reinforcing an audit culture that mimics organizational structures of a market economy. In addition class sizes are ballooning, curriculum is stripped of liberal values, research is largely assessed for its ability to produce profits, administrative staffs are being cut back, governance has been handed over to paragons of corporate culture, and valuable services are being either outsourced or curtailed.[23]

The issues raised by Giroux are unfortunately all too familiar for many of us. The consequences for universities are captured well by Darder who highlights our institutions as,

> . . . the university industrial complex, which has unfolded a wretched instrumentalizing nightmare of marketization and accountability schemes meant to ensure that higher education fulfill its role as a roaring economic engine and military aegis of the capitalist class.[24]

This has consequences, sometimes dire, for academic staff who,

> . . . risk madness to succeed. [. . .] Some become nervous wrecks, worn down by hyper-competitiveness and its adjunct administrivia, while others play possum, default into zombification, passing as undead to survive, desensitised by audit, surveillance, workload, workforce and acquiescence of academic leadership.[25]

The negative impact of marketisation has affected not just staff, but also students. The idea of education as a social good[26] has been stripped away, and combined with the siren call of the market and the arrival of metrics, has been rebranded using the language of student autonomy, freedom of choice and control. Ironically, it is proposed that what is being sold is perceived rather than actual control, and misses the fact that students always had a voice, there was always accountability, but what was relational has now become atomising. Viewed in this way, HE, via the language of the market, has exploited staff and students' shared humanity and vulnerabilities, and in doing so reduced itself as a means to an end rather than an end in itself.

Law schools, clearly successful in neoliberal terms with good student numbers and employability rates, are not immune from the negative impacts outlined above and may even amplify them.[27] In the context of law schools, the impact of neoliberal market forces is stark. The battle for market dominance is reflected via increasingly glitzy open days, real or virtual,[28] the use of law school league tables, coupled with the further increase in marketisation and implied threat to staff of redundancies if Higher Education Funding Council for England (HEFCE) Teaching Excellence Framework (TEF) scores are not Silver or Gold,[29] and the instrumentalisation of the HEFCE's Research Excellence

---

[23]Giroux (n 1) 30, citing Joelle Fanghanel, *Being an Academic* (Routledge 2012).

[24]Angela Darder, "Foreword" in Bottrell and Manathunga (eds) (n 9) v.

[25]Martin Andrew, "Double Negative: When the Neoliberal Meets the Toxic" in Bottrell and Manathunga (eds) (n 9) 59, 71.

[26]The view that education is a social or public good is held by various academics; see for example Jandhyala BG Tilak, "Higher Education: A Public Good or a Commodity Trade?" (2009) 38 Prospects 449.

[27]Anthony Bradney, "The Success of University Law Schools in England and Wales: Or How to Fail" (2018) 52 The Law Teacher 490.

[28]This reflects the current approach to recruitment as a result of the Covid-19 pandemic, and reinforces the marketisation and instrumentalisation of education as an income source.

[29]See for example Mark Leach, "TEF Results – Do the Prizes Still Glitter?" (*WonkHE*, 22 June 2017) https://wonkhe.com/blogs/tef-results-do-the-prizes-still-glitter/ which> accessed 21 September 2020 points to the reduction in fees income which might arise from Bronze TEF or more recently Matt O'Leary, Dr Vanessa Cui and Dr

Framework (REF) which dictates the type of research seen as valuable (or impactful). Furthermore, and perhaps with some irony, our experience suggests that the legal practitioners leaving a culturally demanding and hierarchical profession for a university life have brought with them the very thing they sought to evade: managerial and hierarchical structures. Whilst such cultural appropriation could be viewed as seeking comfort in a strange new world, the reality is less prosaic. The imposition of hierarchical structures and process mimics the firm, serving to concentrate the drivers of neoliberalism. In a misplaced attempt to bring order to what is perceived as chaos, what is revealed is a deep cultural dissonance, between education as a legal product, something to be sold and commodified where staff and students are metrics and education as a social good, where staff and students are intertwined relationally. The idea of instrumentalism implied in the commodification argument is lent further credence by university management's often unquestioning acceptance of change driven by the legal profession. Arguably the most recent example of this is the introduction of the Solicitors Qualifying Exam (SQE)[30] by the Solicitors Regulation Authority (SRA) for England and Wales, along with its impact, the rise of multiple-choice questions (MCQs) into what we would argue is a liberal arts degree.

The impact of the market has served to sever, at least for the moment, the connection between education as a social good and education simply as a means to an end. In the process, this revealed the corrosive impact of the market not only on HE and law schools generally, but also on university staff, and students. To use the language of the market, if their autonomy, choice and voice are to be realised, as well as ours, we need to embrace vulnerability theory. Its adoption would facilitate an open discussion of shared aims and values, by reminding us to ask the fundamental question of what it means to be human.[31] Not only do such discussions serve to remind the organisation and the law school of their responsibilities, e.g., by asking what are "law schools for", but they also remind staff and students of our interdependency, and the shared resilience that such interdependency reveals.[32] Certainly, a liberal law degree, which is in essence what we propose a law degree should be, can (along with vulnerability theory) remind us to ask the question, what does it mean to be human and in doing so provide the means by which our humanity can be cultivated.[33] A discussion we will return to later.

The incorporation of professional drivers reveals the juxtaposition of a market that sells itself as the guardian of student autonomy and choice, and law schools seeking to market themselves as the access point to an increasingly exclusive profession,[34] where choice is really not there for the majority.[35] This view finds traction in figures published by the Law Society of England and Wales, which reveal that undergraduate law students outstrip available training contracts alone by 3:1, whilst overall students entering

---

Amanda French, "Understanding, Recognising and Rewarding Teaching Quality in Higher Education: An Exploration of the Impact and Implications of the Teaching Excellence Framework" (UCU 2019) <www.ucu.org.uk/media/10092/Impact-of-TEF-report-Feb-2019/pdf/ImpactofTEFreportFEb2019> accessed 21 September 2020.

[30]Kathleen Lynch, "Neo-liberalism and Marketisation: The Implications for Higher Education" (2006) 5 European Educational Research Journal 1, 2.

[31]Fineman (n 19) 357.

[32]ibid 368.

[33]See Martha C Nussbaum, *Cultivating Humanity: A Classical Defense of Reform in Liberal Education* (Harvard University Press 2003).

[34]Guth and Dutton (n 4).

[35]ibid.

practice are in the region of 20–25%.[36] The reality for staff and students is the abrogation by the HE sector in general, and law schools in particular, of their responsibilities to engender structures and processes that recognise our shared vulnerabilities, acknowledge our interdependency and our need for resilience, in favour of "profits over people".[37]

Vulnerability in the neoliberal law school: let's rethink

As we suggest above, the neoliberal university presents a series of problems, all linked in complex ways, which highlight our vulnerability and the inadequacies of responses to tackle the impacts of those problems. This section focuses on the extent to which vulnerability theory can help us to reframe some of these issues to allow us to begin thinking about alternative ways of organising academic labour in law schools. It does so on two levels. First it addresses some of the conceptual issues that go to the heart of the neoliberal and marketised law school. Second, and given that it seems highly unlikely that we will be able to halt and reverse the marketisation process,[38] it addresses some of the outcomes or symptoms that result from the current state of higher education generally and law schools specifically.

Reframing the neoliberal law school

The neoliberal and marketised law school is about individual success, defined as highest test scores, highest paying internship or job secured, highest teaching evaluation scores and/or most research money secured. In addition these are seen to be dependent entirely on the individual's ability, on merit and on the individual's actions or inactions. Structures that may disadvantage certain groups of students[39] or staff can be ignored, and inherent inequalities brushed under the carpet, whilst the "absurd hyper-individualism"[40] underpinning much of academia results in students being pitched against each other in a competitive environment. This is often the antithesis to an effective learning environment and encourages staff to focus on short-term, box-ticking and metric-appeasing goals without much reference to the impact that may have on students or colleagues. It is not about them it is about individual success. When staff and students are not able to succeed the failing is theirs. This logic is applied at institutional level in England, playing out in the Russell Group versus New University or academic versus vocationally focused law degrees rhetoric,[41] as well as at an individual level pitching the star researcher against the mere teacher. Vulnerability theory offers a way out of this thinking,

---

[36]See Steven Vaughan, "The Lies We Tell Ourselves: Problematising the (S)Hallow Foundations of the Core of Legal Education" (Society of Legal Scholars Annual Conference, UCLAN, Preston, September 2019).

[37]Noam Chomsky, *Profit Over People: Neoliberalism and Global Order* (Seven Stories Press 1999).

[38]Kathryn Telling, "Different Universities, Different Temporalities: Placing the Acceleration of Academic Life in Context" (2019) 23 Perspectives Policy and Practice in Higher Education 132, 133.

[39]Louise Archer, Merryn Hutchings and Alistair Ross, *Higher Education and Social Class: Issues of Exclusion and Inclusion* (Routledge 2003); Diane Reay, Gill Crozier and John Clayton, "'Fitting In' or 'Standing Out': Working-Class Students in UK Higher Education" (2010) 36 British Educational Research Journal 107; Hilary Sommerlad and others, "The Futures of Legal Education and the Legal Profession" in Hilary Sommerlad and others (eds), *The Futures of Legal Education and the Legal Profession* (Hart 2015). Guth and Dutton (n 4).

[40]Telling (n 38) 133.

[41]Setting these debates out here is beyond the scope of this paper but a search through *The Law Teacher* archives will reveal a wide variety of articles dealing with this issue.

> In a vulnerability analysis, the basis for distinguishing some individuals from better positioned but equally vulnerable individuals in the first instance would revolve around questions of access to sufficient resources, with a deficit indicating they lacked the resilience that is necessary to address human vulnerability. Significantly, the initial emphasis here is on the distribution or allocation of resources and the structures within which they are produced. This suggests that the first question to be considered is whether institutional, not individual, functioning is inadequate.[42]

A vulnerability analysis therefore means that the different contexts in which law schools operate and their different missions give rise to different interdependencies and expose their inhabitants to different vulnerabilities. It is not that some are more or less vulnerable in a sense that suggests better or worse but simply that they are differently vulnerable and susceptible to change in different ways – being affected more or less by different factors and changes in context and environment. The current legal education reforms in England and Wales provides a useful example. While the changes proposed by the SRA in the form of the SQE are not likely to have an impact on the structures, workload or general running of those law schools thought of as elite, the impact is likely to be significant for those law schools traditionally focused on a more vocational approach to legal education.[43]

A vulnerability analysis here suggests that in order to take account of the vulnerabilities of the students and academics at those institutions these differences and differential interdependencies need to be recognised. We should call for a different allocation of resources depending on how those interdependencies between the law school and its students, the law school and its staff, the law school and the legal services sector and the law school and the general employment market as well as between staff and students play out in those different contexts. This is not, to be absolutely clear, an argument for teaching-only institutions or positions or for funded research to be concentrated in only so-called elite institutions or research centres. Instead it is a recognition that in order for all university law schools to offer their particular flavour of legal education in a positive way, there has to be space within the regulation, resourcing and structuring of law schools to support those differences and to reduce so far as is possible any disadvantage suffered because students study at or staff work for a particular institution or type of institution. These issues are structural and require a structural and collective rather than managerial solution. It is not the functioning of the individual but the functioning of the institution, both in the sense of the sector overall and individual law schools, that is inadequate and thus preventing all law students and all legal academics from surviving and thriving. Applying vulnerability theory at this conceptual level then would suggest that collectively we should be arguing for law schools which are structured in such a way which allows for the allocation and distribution of resources that empower staff to create effective learning environments[44] which are inclusive and support staff and students in their development, recognising their differing vulnerabilities and staff and students' dependencies on each other. We should therefore be arguing that law schools, and their structures and processes,

[42]Fineman, "Vulnerability and Inevitable Inequality" (n 14) 147.

[43]See for example the responses to the SRA's application to the Legal Services Board from the Learned Subject Associations <http://lawteacher.ac.uk/alt-policy/letr-and-sqe/> accessed 20 September 2020.

[44]This cooperation is most needed at the time of writing as universities shift to online learning in response to the Covid-19 pandemic. However, the reality is that academics are being told to "simply shift stuff online", with no thought for the pedagogical drivers or how much work is actually needed. Rather than pedagogy, money (or more importantly the potential loss of money) is the driver.

recognise staff as vulnerable and therefore support staff to carry out their roles in a way which means something to them and which aligns their values to those of the institution.[45] If we accept that "Vulnerability theory is more focused on establishing the parameters of state responsibility for societal intuitions and relationships than it is on setting the limits of state intervention"[46] then the parameters in which the organisation and structure of law schools and legal education take place must account for differences between the purpose and mission of different law schools and ensure that any disadvantages resulting from those differences are minimised. This approach might not seem that radical but it runs counter to the culture of ranking, metrics and audit. Vulnerability theory lets us rethink the use of metrics and excellence rhetoric and focus on relationships and interdependencies. Instead of asking about overall satisfaction with courses, or value of research grants for example, vulnerability analysis encourages us to look at the human interactions that sit behind those metrics. What becomes important is the way staff can become a source of resilience for students and for each other, the way all students can be supported to achieve their potential through the provision of materials, guidance and learning opportunities best suited to their needs, the way academics can draw on materials, time and space provided by institutions in order to develop their teaching, scholarship and research and the way in which institutions acknowledge and react to these interdependencies and vulnerabilities.[47]

Moving away from metrics though is difficult. The metrics feed the league tables which are so inextricably linked with student recruitment which, as mentioned, appears to be linked to the survival of departments and in some cases institutions highlighting the vulnerability of universities as institutions. This has been exacerbated by the introduction of significant tuition fees and the, often unrealistic or ill-founded, student expectations that go with that. In the context of England and Wales tuition fees have increased since the introduction of modest fees in 1998 to a level which now saddles graduates with significant debt, and which opens the door to possible financial regulation or at least incentives as to which subjects are studied by students and therefore offered by universities. Law schools do well in this model.[48] The marketisation of HE has witnessed the commodification of the degree and law degrees remain a valuable and sought-after commodity. Students are told they are consumers, they pay for their degrees (rather than the opportunity to study), they have rights and expect certain outcomes.[49] In the context of law schools, expectations of what happens throughout the degree, which topics are studied and which are not and significantly, what has to be "done" in order to achieve the highest grade, are often linked to expectations of access to high paying jobs in a narrowly defined legal sector. This is something which remains out of reach for most.[50] A vulnerability analysis again allows us to challenge the narrative of metrics and consider the situation of students and their recruitment differently.

---

45 Recognising here also that this may not be possible but that a vulnerability analysis would suggest that the institution needs to respond and either change or support staff in being able to find alternative roles within the institution or the sector more widely leading to a more responsive sector overall.

46 Martha Albertson Fineman, "Beyond Equality and Discrimination" (2020) 73 SMU L Rev F 51, 61.

47 The use of metrics is contested by various academics, but for a more recent example see Matt O'Leary and Phil Wood, "Reimagining Teaching Excellence: Why Collaboration, Rather than Competition, Holds the Key to Improving Teaching and Learning in Higher Education" (2019) 71 Educational Review 122.

48 Bradney (n 27).

49 Lynch (n 30); Collini (n 1).

50 Guth and Dutton (n 4).

Importantly, the use of such metrics tells us something about what is valued in the current system and it is not difficult to draw lines between the metrics, increasing student expectations and increasing staff workloads induced by demands of increased contact time, quicker marking turnarounds and more tightly controlled and standardised interactions. The introduction of higher student fees, the removal of the student cap, the maximisation of student recruitment, the metrics examining student satisfaction, continuation and employment outcomes[51] alongside the REF pressure to produce impactful research, win grant income, publish world-leading outputs as well as disseminate knowledge outside the academy and give back to the community place ever-increasing pressure on academic staff. These pressures vary greatly depending on type of institution, role and seniority but across the sector academics are seen as human resources, as an expense in the production and delivery of products which consumers can then choose to purchase or engage with. With staff being seen as a resource only, the casualisation of the academic workforce is evidenced through the normalisation of non-standard contracts, their seemingly gendered use, and the commodification of academics, as exemplified by the use of management language, such as "units of cost".[52] The use of such language serves to dehumanise and further pitches academic staff against each other in competition for secure jobs, promotions or roles which better align with their ambitions or values. The result for the individual is increased workload, a fear of saying no which is matched only by the fear of failure defined as poor evaluation scores, publication rejections or not getting a grant, and risking being a jack of all trades but master of none.

Vulnerability theory can help rethink these problems too. Academics are vulnerable, susceptible to the changing demands of students, and the often unrealistic expectations of the law schools within which they work (which in turn are also vulnerable and dependent on the overall institution). If we accept this, then we must require the law schools, individually, through their institutions and as a sector to provide access to resources for staff to allow us to cope with the demands. This means rethinking structures, including dealing with questions around what proportion of income should be spent on staffing and what that staff body should look like in terms of permanent versus casual staff, in terms of seniority and in terms of skills and expertise. It would ask us to think carefully about staff/student ratios, organisation of work, time allocated for tasks on workload planning/allocation models. Looking at academic work and how it is organised from a vulnerability perspective is likely to, implicitly perhaps, suggest that more focus must be given to increasing staff numbers. Resources and structures which favour building projects and marketing brochures over ensuring sufficient members of staff to allow all work to be carried out without doing harm to staff are ill-founded and unjustifiable. Vulnerability theory leads us to think more about how a law school and its success are dependent on the individuals which make up the law school and therefore the law school as an institution must be structured in a way which allows those individuals to thrive, individually and

[51] Office for Students, "TEF Data" <http://www.officeforstudents.org.uk/advice-and-guidance/teaching/tef-data/>accessed 26 September 2019.

[52] UCU (University and College Union), "Precarious Work in Higher Education: A Snapshot of Insecure Contracts and Institutional Attitudes" (April 2016) <https://www.ucu.org.uk/media/7995/Precarious-work-in-higher-education-a-snapshot-of-insecure-contracts-and-institutional-attitudes-Apr-16/pdf/ucu_precariouscontract_hereport_apr16.pdf> accessed 27 May 2020; Stefan Collini, "Covid-19 Shows up UK Universities' Shameful Employment Practices" *The Guardian* (London, 28 April 2020) <www.theguardian.com/education/2020/apr/28/covid-19-shows-up-uk-universities-shameful-employment-practices> accessed 27 May 2020.

collectively. As Fineman notes, "Just as no individual can successfully stand apart from the state and its institutions, the destiny of the state ultimately relies on the actions of the individuals who constitute it."[53] Exactly the same can be said for law schools.

Using vulnerability theory now

We have made some suggestions as to how vulnerability theory can help us rethink and address some of the issues raised by the marketisation of law schools. However, while this reframing and rethinking is a useful exercise at a theoretical level and can help move us towards advocating policy change at individual law school and university level as well as more broadly for the sector, it is not of much help for legal academics, like us, who are caught up in the day-to-day of academia, firefighting competing demands in an increasingly stretched system. Building on this we will now consider the extent to which vulnerability theory can help us with thinking about addressing some of the outcomes or symptoms of the neoliberal law school. Telling has noted that "whilst the problems may be structural, any workable response will be at the level of individual (self) management"[54] and this is an attractive suggestion. Of course something which is going to make our lives as legal academics better and more meaningful will have to happen at the individual level. However, "vulnerability theory has the power to disrupt the logic of personal responsibility and individual liberty built on the liberal stereotype of an independent and autonomous individual"[55] and this section tries to do that in two areas. We deal first with the question of overwork and burnout and then with questions of job satisfaction.

We have already outlined issues of increasing staff workload and student demand and this has, not surprisingly, led to a mental health crisis in law schools. An almost universal vulnerability among legal academics is overwork, burnout and mental ill health manifesting in depression and/or anxiety.[56] Law schools are not unaware of this and respond, at departmental or faculty level as well as tapping into university responses. It can be argued that universities provide the resources to inculcate resilience and to build meaningful relationships by offering wellness courses, mental health training, lunchtime yoga and walks or mindfulness sessions alongside, in some cases, conference, workshops, seminar series and occasionally more social get-togethers. However, these sessions reflect not organisational concern for employees, but an organisation obsessed with ticking boxes and placing responsibility on individuals. As Morrish writes, "universities have sought to mitigate their legal liability by offering employees enhanced access to 'wellness solutions'".[57]

Resilience for law schools is more Cartesian, a way to sidestep responsibility and a means of placing the locus of responsibility back on to the individual staff member and to tightly control the sort of supportive relationships we seek to build. The following is a familiar feeling for many colleagues: in spite of all of the resources you have access too, the lunchtime yoga, the mindfulness sessions and subsidised gym memberships, you

[53]Fineman (n 46) 62.
[54]Telling (n 38) 132.
[55]Fineman (n 46) 54.
[56]Liz Morrish, "Pressure Vessels" (HEPI Occasional Paper 20, 2019).
[57]Morrish (n 56) 39. See also David Webster and Nicola Rivers, "Critiquing Discourses of Resilience in Education" (*Fruits of the Pedagogic Life*, 14 May 2017) <https://davewebster.org/2017/05/14/a-contrary-view-critiquing-discourses-of-resilience-in-education/> accessed 20 September 2020.

are not resilient enough and the fact that the networks we force you into do not sustain you intellectually or emotionally is of course also your fault. The provision of wellbeing services, perhaps despite best efforts, serves further to atomise; failure is individual and personal, whilst solutions are individual rather than organisational and relational. Viewed in this way vulnerability is ignored and wellbeing services and their staff become an adjunct of the organisation, the aim being to ensure the "smooth running of the organisation".[58] In other words, the institutional response to vulnerability is neoliberal and market driven and focused on individuals taking responsibility for failure or failing to cope rather than on changing structures which initially created the environment where our vulnerability has a negative impact.

Vulnerability can help us to understand that it is the structures that are the problem and can help us think about how different structures might better address the issue of overwork and burnout but it cannot help us to actually reduce our workload. Some of us might be in positions where we can access more resources and be more resilient to the pressures of work, we might be better able to say no, better able to align our work with law school goals, research in areas which currently attract funding or teach courses students like and do well in. However that does not mean that even those in the least vulnerable positions are not susceptible to the threat of not getting a promotion, losing a job or having to do work, perhaps even the majority of our work, which gives us little satisfaction, nor does it stop us from having to spend too much of our time having to do the work we are expected, some might say contracted to do. Expecting a legal academic teaching 14 hours a week across 4 subjects, looking after 50 personal tutees, supervising several postgraduate students and maintaining a research and/or scholarship workload to spend significant time and energies challenging the overall structures at play in a department, university or the sector is not realistic.[59] Most of us are too caught up in surviving the day-to-day. Therefore on an individual and practical level, vulnerability theory does not help us get through the day.[60]

The second area in which we wish to think about the practical application of vulnerability theory is job satisfaction. There are many factors which shape job satisfaction: the meaning the work carries for us, the amount of control we have over our own work and structuring our time, the benefit of our work to others, the salary and other benefits, the security and perhaps the intellectual challenge it brings. Academics, while perhaps not badly paid, are not highly paid compared to those with similar qualifications in the private sector and other benefits such as pensions have been under sustained attack. There are few perks, at least in financial terms, to being an academic. The impact of neoliberalism has witnessed the rise of managerialism and the decrease in collective and collegiate decision-making, in essence localised atomism over shared decision-making, law school autonomy, at least relationally, is no more. The amount of control academics have over their working lives has been reduced along with the amount of freedom we have to research and to teach in ways which follows our

[58] Telling (n 38) 133.

[59] While this is a hypothetical based on our own experience and the experience of colleagues at a variety of institutions, there is evidence of workloads changing and increasing. See for example O'Leary and others (n 29). See <http://www.timeshighereducation.com/features/paid-research-time-vanishing-privilege-modern-academics>accessed 18 September 2020.

[60] It must be noted that in UK universities there is the opportunity for a collective response for example via engagement with the University College Union (UCU), professional groups or of course codes of ethics. The issue here is that this is time consuming for someone who may not have such time for the reasons discussed. However, they remain an option.

interests. The marketised law school also places increasing emphasis on an employability agenda which privileges so-called graduate jobs and high paying professions[61] and focuses student expectations on employment and salaries rather than on learning as the primary goal. With students focused on what they need to do to pass in order to get a job and law schools and the institutions they sit within focused on meeting their key performance indicators the values of both students and institutions often seem ill aligned with the values and expectations of academics who tend to be more focused on education for education's sake and who may want to pursue research which does not fit the current impact agenda, does not bring in research money and does not lend itself to being featured in a glossy magazine or on a flashy blog. The adoption of market principles and the language of the student consumer ignores that universities are at least in part a public service, with public service values,[62] whilst the language has ushered in not simply a competing value system, but one which is in some respects diametrically opposed to academic values. Job satisfaction and wellbeing are directly linked to the extent to which our values align with those of our employers and the work that we do. It is therefore perhaps not surprising that job satisfaction for academics is dropping and that there is significant mental ill health and a general lack of wellbeing among academics in law schools.[63]

Given that, how does or can vulnerability theory help? On the one level vulnerability theory can help us to articulate a clear message to the HE sector, and therefore law schools, that they must recognise and respond to our vulnerabilities and our shared humanity, and provide the structures and processes through which our resilience can be enhanced. However, vulnerability theory does not, on a practical level, provide us with tools to help us deal with misaligned values and differing expectations. It cannot deal with the cultural dissonance or with the frustration many feel because the theory as it stands has not been able to move beyond the theoretical challenge to the practical one that is posed by current law schools, HE structures and values. Thinking differently about issues might be the starting point to but it is very different from actually instituting change. At this point, the value of vulnerability theory comes from its theoretical power to reframe rather than from any practical application that can be harnessed to make a tangible difference in how we live our academic lives and give them meaning right now.[64]

Concluding thoughts

Vulnerability theory allows us to think differently about the ills of the neoliberal university by shifting the focus away from academics as individuals trying to

---

[61] For this argument in the context of skills teaching see Jessica Guth, "The Past and Future of Legal Skills Teaching" in Emma Jones and Fiona Cownie (eds), *Key Directions in Legal Education: National and International Perspectives* (Routledge 2020).

[62] David Kernohan, "Who Decides the Future of Universities?" (*WonkHE*, Comment, 22 May 2020) <wonkhe.com> accessed 27 May 2020.

[63] See Wilson and Strevens (n 7).

[64] While vulnerability theory cannot help us make a practical difference to our academic lives in the overall everyday, it can of course be utilised to help make a difference in some aspects of our academic lives. We see examples of the theory being drawn on to set up projects in different and more responsive ways across a variety of legal and educational arenas and the Vulnerability and the Human Condition Initiative website provides a plethora of published examples at <https://web.gs.emory.edu/vulnerability/resources/publications.html> accessed 28 May 2020.

survive in the system either by assimilating and embracing marketisation or by resisting and pushing back in defence of education and academic freedom. Instead it invites us to think about the failings of the state overall and universities more specifically to engage with the vulnerabilities, the susceptibility to change to use Fineman's basic definition,[65] we all have. Vulnerability theory allows us to examine the empirical reality of academic lives and argue that the structures which influence and shape our experiences are inadequate. Our collective experience clearly demonstrates that current ways of doing legal education – as academics or students – do damage and reinforce rather than reduce inequalities. Vulnerability makes us stop and challenge the assumptions that this is the fault of those individuals struggling within the system. Instead we can focus on structures, rules, regulations and cultures which stop us from accessing what we require in order to organise our academic labour in ways which are both healthier and more equal. However, the structural barriers which are arguably so problematic and which are brought into focus by focusing on vulnerability are arguably also the structures which make it so difficult to utilise vulnerability to mobilise solutions. The marketisation of the university sector means that universities are often not providing "assets or resources that enable us to survive, and even thrive, within society"[66] because collaboration, collegiality and support stand in sometimes stark contrast to competition, individualism and perceived excellence. The structures within which we work no longer encourage or sometimes even allow meaningful relationships and positive interdependencies which would help us support each other and produce meaningful work. Vulnerability is sometimes used, Fineman warns, "to stigmatise",[67] and vulnerable people or in this instance vulnerable academic staff are simply "suffering the just results of their own individual failures".[68] This atomisation of vulnerability results in the law school's focus on the individual, rather than on the organisational and structural issues which may have facilitated or exacerbated this. In other words, unsurprisingly the neoliberal law school's response to challenge from vulnerability theory is neoliberal in essence. In order to utilise vulnerability theory at a practical level, significant reclaiming of both vulnerability as something inherent and constant as well as resilience as something predominantly dependent on access to resources and empowering structures is necessary. Viewed from this perspective, vulnerability theory is aspirational and struggles to move away from an, albeit important, reframing and towards providing tools which can be operationalised now to make a difference in our lives and create space to allow us to advocate more structural and overall change in the longer term. Paradoxically this might mean that those with vulnerabilities which must most urgently be addressed, those on limited time or hourly contracts, those suffering mental ill health because of workload issues or pressures to demonstrate excellence or those overwhelmed with students requiring support for their complex vulnerabilities will never be in positions where they are able to make their voices heard and where their

[65]Fineman (n 14).
[66]Fineman (n 14) 146.
[67]Martha Albertson Fineman, "The Vulnerable Subject and the Responsive State" (2010) 60 Emory Law Journal 251, 266.
[68]Martha Albertson Fineman, "The Vulnerable Subject: Anchoring Equality in the Human Condition" (2008) 20 Yale Journal of Law and Feminism 1, 18.

vulnerabilities will be taken into account. While a vulnerability analysis suggests that those of us who can, should consider those vulnerabilities and work to understand and react to those interdependencies and address them, our lived experience shows how unlikely this is for most people most of the time. The problem with Fineman's theory is not in its aspiration or in its usefulness in challenging dominant and harmful ways of thinking about academic labour in neoliberal law schools, but in its application to our everyday work here and now before any of the structural changes needed can be brought about, if they ever can.[69] If we are to achieve more meaningful academic lives collectively, we need more.

Disclosure statement

No potential conflict of interest was reported by the authors.

[69]See Morgan Cloud, "More than Utopia" in Martha Albertson Fineman and Anna Grear, *Vulnerability Reflections on a New Ethical Foundation for Law and Politics* (Ashgate 2013) 70.

Vulnerability, the future of the criminal defence profession, and the implications for teaching and learning

Nicola Harris, Roxanna Dehaghani and Daniel Newman

ABSTRACT

Legally aided criminal defence work is under significant strain at present following fee stagnations and funding cuts over the last 20 years. This has obvious implications for those working in criminal defence practice, which have been examined in the literature on access to criminal justice. However, the implications for teaching and learning within criminal law and practice have been not been subject to much attention. Within we reflect on the teaching and learning challenges. Further, we use a Fineman vulnerability analysis to illustrate how the challenges faced by criminal defence practice – in the face of a crumbling criminal justice system – affect criminal law and process teaching and learning. Finally, we explore how the resilience of criminal defence can be provided (or bolstered) by and within the academe.

Introduction

In earlier work, Newman and Dehaghani explored the vulnerability of criminal legal aid lawyers and the institutions within which they work.[1] We argued that legally aided criminal defence lawyers (and, in our specific paper, solicitors), by virtue of being human, were vulnerable, but that this vulnerability was particularly heightened within the conditions of austerity and neoliberalism. Using vulnerability theory, we suggested that the resilience of criminal defence lawyers and the institutions of justice within which they work has been reduced through cuts to criminal legal aid, as a result of the wider austerity agenda. Following on from this, we received funding to further interview criminal defence lawyers (both solicitors and barristers) on the impact of cuts.[2] We found that there were concerns regarding the future of the criminal defence profession, or at least of a profession that was publicly funded. In this paper we take this analysis and debate one step further: we consider how the demise of the criminal defence profession may have an impact upon students who are studying law, specifically those

---

[1]Roxanna Dehaghani and Daniel Newman, "'We're Vulnerable Too': An (Alternative) Analysis of Vulnerability within English Criminal Legal Aid and Police Custody" (2017) 7 Oñati Socio-Legal Series 1199.

[2]This work is ongoing and will be published as Daniel Newman and Roxanna Dehaghani, *Experiences of Criminal Justice: Perspectives from Wales on a System in Crisis* (Bristol University Press 2021). British Academy Grant, Ref: SRG\170958.

who have aspirations to go into criminal practice, and we further reflect on our position as academics teaching criminal law and the criminal process at undergraduate and postgraduate level (specifically on the LLB and the BTC).[3] In doing so we highlight the self-supportive and self-undermining vulnerabilities of the criminal legal profession, students, and academics. We focus specifically on whether and how academics and universities can provide resilience to our students and to the profession within which our students may wish to work. We further examine whether the university has a role – and what that role may be – in resisting the neoliberal demise of the criminal defence profession.

Within this paper, we utilise vulnerability theory to argue for an institutional response to the demise of the criminal defence profession. In particular, we query whether university leaders – in pursuance of their aim to ensure opportunities for students and, perhaps more obviously, in pursuance of their civic mission – should be doing more to support the criminal defence profession. We begin by looking at the criminal defence profession. We highlight the importance of criminal lawyers, and the challenges faced by solicitors and barristers in practice. Next, we explore our own experience of teaching criminal law and procedure to students. We consider our teaching against the tough reality of life in criminal practice. We then move on to the ethics of teaching criminal law and procedure in this context. With all we know about how difficult criminal practice can be, we need to reflect on what and how we teach students. Thereafter, we focus on our academic and institutional obligations. Here we draw out the value of vulnerability theory in helping us to understand the role we could and should play to tackle the challenges that criminal lawyers face in practice. We conclude by highlighting the role that universities can play in providing resilience. Bolstering criminal defence is not a duty to be left to us as individual academics; it is something that the academe more widely should support.

The criminal defence profession: current problems and the shaky future

Legally aided criminal defence lawyers are crucial for access to justice in an adversarial system (as operates in England and Wales). Access to criminal justice requires that suspects and defendants can effectively participate in the case against them, enforce their fair trial rights, and ensure that they can mount an effective defence against the state. Not only should the state be required to prove its case against the defendant beyond reasonable doubt and by the procedures laid down in law, it is also required that the defendant can get a fair trial by, for example, having access to effective criminal defence. The right to a fair trial is enshrined in Article 6 of the European Convention on Human Rights and includes the right to have adequate time and facilities for the preparation of the defence, and the right to defend oneself in person or through legal assistance of the defendant's choosing. On the right to defend oneself, Article 6 also requires that legal assistance be provided for free when the defendant does not have sufficient means to pay for legal assistance themselves (albeit with the caveat: when the interests of justice so require). This right extends to

[3]The LLB or Bachelor of Laws degree is the primary undergraduate law degree in England and Wales and an example of a qualifying law degree (QLD). The BTC (Bar Training Course), previously the BPTC (Bar Professional Training Course), is a specific one-year postgraduate qualification allowing students to progress to be called to the Bar as part of the process of qualification as a barrister.

pre-trial procedures,[4] and requires that the state provide legal advice and assistance to those who are suspected of committing a criminal offence.[5]

The role of lawyers here can be found from the way the defendant can be faced with a confusing, complicated environment once drawn into the criminal justice system. Carlen has shown how the criminal courts function as a form of social control to render defendants as "dummy players",[6] while McBarnet documents the way that criminal courts "alienate" defendants.[7] In the face of this, defendants can quickly find themselves very much out of their comfort zone – left inarticulate and overwhelmed. As such, it seems necessary to provide them with a helping hand to guide them through: an expert. It is at this point that the notion of the equality of arms assumes its significance: the adversarial system depends on there being powerful arguments on both sides of the question of legal guilt. On their own, defendants would face a permanent, and telling, disadvantage against the might of the state. To avoid this, they should be provided with access to criminal defence practitioners: lawyers. Accordingly, Goriely outlines the "unequivocally" held principle that "in the adversarial system which prevails in the courts in this country, representation is needed on both sides".[8] Indeed, McConville and others consider that "the need for defendants to be legally represented in criminal cases is perhaps so obvious that the fact that solicitors may be seen giving advice at the police stations to suspects who have been arrested and advocating their cause in Magistrates' Courts hardly seems to require explanation".[9] The reality is that most defendants simply cannot afford to hire a criminal defence lawyer privately. As such, access to justice does not simply require access to criminal defence lawyers but, specifically, requires access to criminal defence lawyers funded by legal aid.[10] Indeed, for Ashworth, the ability to defend oneself should not depend on financial resources.[11] Following Young and Wall, "access to justice seems, therefore, to imply access to legal aid and lawyers",[12] and such is the position we take in this paper.[13]

Such access to justice, though, is under threat as, per the Law Society, the English and Welsh criminal justice system is "crumbling",[14] in large part due to underfunding,

[4]*Teixeira de Castro v Portugal* (1998) 28 EHRR 101.
[5]*Salduz v Turkey* (2009) 49 EHRR 19.
[6]Pat Carlen, *Magistrates' Justice* (Martin Robertson 1976).
[7]Doreen J McBarnet, *Conviction: Law, the State and the Construction of Justice* (Palgrave Macmillan 1981).
[8]Tamara Goriely, "The Development of Criminal Legal Aid in England and Wales" in Richard Young and David Wall (eds), *Access to Criminal Justice* (Blackstone Press 1996) 26.
[9]Michael McConville and others, *Standing Accused* (Oxford University Press 1994) 2.
[10]There is no public defender service in England and Wales.
[11]Andrew Ashworth, "Legal Aid, Human Rights and Criminal Justice" in Richard Young and David Wall (eds), *Access to Criminal Justice* (Blackstone Press 1996).
[12]Richard Young and David Wall, "Criminal Justice, Legal Aid and the Defence of Liberty" in Richard Young and David Wall (eds), *Access to Criminal Justice* (Blackstone Press 1996) 6.
[13]The text assumes the absence of a US-style public defender service whereby a lawyer directly employed by the state or federal government is provided to all those who cannot afford a private lawyer rather than the judicare model of private practice bidding for legal aid contracts that predominates in England and Wales. Such schemes had influenced the New Labour approach to cost-cutting in criminal legal aid as they suggested that evidence from other countries promised that properly funded salaried defenders could be more cost-effective (and provide a better service) than lawyers in private practice. A salaried Public Defender Service was piloted in England and Wales in 2001 but, as it did not meet government expectations, only four remain, including two in Wales (Pontypridd and Swansea).
[14]Law Society, "Justice on Trial 2019: Fixing Our Criminal Justice System" (Law Society 2019).

following years of cuts to public services.[15] The cuts within the criminal justice system have been substantial: under the coalition government, the Ministry of Justice budget (which includes legal aid) fell by 29%; the Ministry of Justice experienced the most significant of funding cuts during the period of austerity (of £4.5bn – from £10.9bn to £6.4bn).[16] Further, in the years 2012/13 to 2017/18 legal aid spending (civil and criminal) dropped from £2.2bn to £1.6bn with criminal legal aid fees stagnating throughout the neoliberal era (from the mid-1990s onwards) and being cut by 8.75% under austerity in 2014.

Criminal defence work is known for not being particularly well remunerated and has always been viewed as such,[17] particularly compared with other areas of legal practice.[18] Yet, figures from the Law Society would indicate that criminal defence solicitors are now in a particularly dire situation, having received no fee increase since 1998.[19] At the same time, house prices and the cost of living have sky-rocketed: for example, since 1998 the average house price here in Wales has trebled (£48,294 to £162,374) such that the fees that practitioners receive are actually worth less than they were 20 years ago.[20] Opportunities, at the same time, seem to be dwindling; a recent parliamentary question to the UK Secretary of State for Justice illustrated the decline of criminal legal aid provision across England and Wales: in 2010/11, 1861 firms and 2598 offices were in operation across England and Wales, whereas in 2018/19 this had declined to 1271 firms and 1921 offices. When compared with the start of austerity (in 2010), there are almost a third fewer criminal legal aid firms in operation, and a quarter fewer offices that offer advice and representation. The Covid-19 pandemic is posing even further challenges for the criminal defence profession: a press release from the Law Society on 17 June 2020 announced that 120 firms had already collapsed as a result of the pandemic.[21]

Similar challenges face the Criminal Bar. Repeated cuts in real terms have been made to payments whilst the burdens placed on practitioners have increased. Over a third of criminal barristers are considering other careers, while a third say they would leave the Bar if they were able to.[22] In its response to the Ministry of Justice's consultation on legal aid and measures in reaction to Covid-19, the Criminal Bar Association recently put matters succinctly: "the financial pressures caused by Covid–19, together with the cumulative effect of deleterious policies is, without exaggeration, the greatest threat the

[15]See Fabian Society, "The Right to Justice: The Final Report of the Bach Commission" (2017). See also Young Legal Aid Lawyers, "Young Legal Aid Lawyers: Social Mobility in a Time of Austerity" (2018) <www.younglegalaidlawyers.org/sites/default/files/Soc%20Mob%20Report%20-%20edited.pdf> accessed 28 January 2020.

[16]Owen Bowcott, "Legal Aid Fees to Be Cut by 8.75%, Confirms Ministry of Justice" *The Guardian* (London, 10 June 2015) <https://www.theguardian.com/law/2015/jun/10/legal-aid-fees-to-be-cut-by-875-confirms-ministry-of-justice>.

[17]Hilary Sommerlad, "Criminal Legal Aid Reforms and the Restructuring of Legal Professionalism" in Richard Young and David Wall (eds), *Access to Criminal Justice: Legal Aid, Lawyers and the Defence of Liberty* (Blackstone Press 1996); Daniel Newman, "More than Money" in J Robins (ed), *No Defence: Lawyers and Miscarriages of Justice* (Wilmington Publishing 2013).

[18]Law Society, "Criminal Duty Solicitors: A Looming Crisis" (2018).

[19]Jared Lawthom, "Law Society Warns Duty Solicitors Could Become Extinct" (*BBC News*, 17 November 2018) <https://www.bbc.co.uk/news/uk-wales-46127118>.

[20]Legal Aid Scheme: Companies: Written Question – 227146 <www.parliament.uk/business/publications/written-questions-answers-statements/written-question/Commons/2019-02-28/227146/> accessed 26 July 2020.

[21]Law Society, Press Release (17 June 2020) <www.lawsociety.org.uk/contact-or-visit-us/press-office/press-releases/120-criminal-firms-have-collapsed-with-more-to-follow> accessed 26 July 2020.

[22]Bar Council, "Barristers' Working Lives 2017" (May 2018) <https://www.barcouncil.org.uk/uploads/assets/694001c1-7e81-4f21-8709602e7d9238ee/working-lives-2017.pdf> accessed 25 January 2021.

Criminal Bar has ever faced".[23] The impact of Covid-related problems falls disproportionately on publicly funded barristers and the Young Bar. A recent survey of the Bar conducted by the Bar Council found that 69% of barristers up to 7 years in practice cannot survive at the Bar for a year without financial help and only 22% of those 0–2 years in practice will survive more than a year. In terms of the Criminal Bar in general, Criminal barristers said they had suffered a 75% reduction in fee income; 38% of criminal barristers were uncertain whether they would renew their practising certificate in 2021 (i.e. whether they would continue in practice).[24]

With fewer firms and offices in operation, with fewer criminal practitioners and pupillages, there will be fewer opportunities for graduates wishing to pursue criminal defence work. Those who do initially engage in criminal defence work are being tempted away by the higher fees earned in areas such as local authority work. In our ongoing research with criminal lawyers, solicitors were reluctant to encourage students and graduates to enter the criminal defence profession because "they'll always be poor"; with barristers going so far as to say that they would actively discourage their children from entering the criminal defence profession. Added to this is the average age of the criminal duty solicitor, which is steadily rising particularly outside large urban areas: almost half of duty solicitors in England and Wales are over the age of 50 and in rural areas this figure creeps up to two thirds. Further, in Wales under 5% of criminal duty solicitors are under the age of 35.[25] Whilst on the face of it, this may not pose problems for those *entering* the profession, it does raise concerns about whether there are enough solicitors to train and mentor those joining the profession. Further, concerns have been raised as to whether criminal defence, as a profession, is sustainable,[26] particularly if those currently in the profession are reaching the age of retirement and there are fewer entering the profession to replace them. Added to this problem is the general decline of state welfare provision and "antipathy … to procedural justice and fair trial".[27]

Whilst these cuts undoubtedly have an impact upon those who are using the criminal justice system – and attempting to access justice – and those who work as criminal defence practitioners, they also affect those who are hoping to enter the criminal defence profession: in other words, (some of) our students. In the section that follows we examine the ways in which the resilience of our students may be affected by wider trends within criminal justice and, in particular, legally aided criminal defence.

Teaching criminal law and criminal procedure

Criminal law and criminal procedure form a part of the syllabus across all institutions offering a qualifying law degree (the academic stage of legal education) at

---

[23]Criminal Bar Association of England and Wales, "Response to The Ministry of Justice Consultation: The Criminal Legal Aid Review & Accelerated Asks" (29 May 2020) <www.criminalbar.com/wp-content/uploads/2020/05/CBA-consultation-Response-CLAR-29.05.20.pdf> accessed 21 July 2020.

[24]The Bar Council, "Whole Bar Survey July 2020" <www.barcouncil.org.uk/uploads/assets/4fb6e80c-5e2c-4cb3-859547bf9f82d946/Bar-Survey-Summary-Findings-July-2020.pdf> accessed 28 July 2020.

[25]Law Society (n 18).

[26]See also James Thornton, "Is Publicly Funded Criminal Defence Sustainable? Legal Aid Cuts, Morale, Retention and Recruitment in the English Criminal Law Professions" (2020) 40 Legal Studies 230.

[27]Tom Smith and Ed Cape, "The Rise and Decline of Criminal Legal Aid in England and Wales" in Asher Flynn and Jacqueline Hodgson (eds), *Access to Justice and Legal Aid: Comparative Perspectives on Unmet Legal Need* (Hart 2017) 63.

undergraduate level across England and Wales. The study of the substantive criminal law has always been a necessary component of the qualifying law degree, and both criminal law and criminal procedure will form a (relatively small) part of the proposed Solicitors Qualifying Examination.[28] The broader extent to which criminal law and procedure and the surrounding areas of research and study form part of the curriculum of the law degree varies from institution to institution, but most offer a variety of optional modules, often incorporating elements of criminology. In Cardiff we choose to also include contextual and socio-legal background in our first year Criminal Law module, with a particular emphasis on the incorporation of feminist perspectives.

Besides being a necessary part of the degree, crime is an often considered an attractive area of study to many students. Students often report to us enjoying crime more than many of their other core subjects, partly because they can engage with the issues and it provides a subject-matter that maintains their interest. Further, when members of the public think of "law", the first images that will spring to a significant proportion of minds are those of the adversarial courtroom, the bewigged barristers and the tales of bloodcurdling offences. It is an area of law which easily captures the imagination and enthusiasm, at least at a superficial level.

For us as educators, teaching criminal law and criminal procedure reflects and concentrates many of the broader issues involved in teaching law. We must set our teaching against this background reminding ourselves why we teach law and why our students study it. The tensions involved in the role of the law school, in particular the perceived duality between the professions and the academe, are well documented.[29] Whilst we may teach so that our students learn to explore the richness and complexity of law and notions of justice within their social, political and historical context, we cannot be blind to the fact that many of our students come to us because they want to become lawyers and see their degree as one step on the path to practice. In a quick survey of our first-year students in a criminal law lecture we found that 85% of students intended to go into legal practice,[30] and that the second most common theme in answer to the question "Why did you decide to study law?" related to employability, career prospects or a specified desire to become a lawyer.[31]

Increasingly the political and public rhetoric frames the "value" of a degree in simple economic terms; indeed the terms of reference for the Augar Review into post-18 education and funding explicitly referenced "value for money".[32] Whilst recent work such as that of Nicholson explores and evaluates the notion of "value" in this context more holistically,[33] we need to acknowledge that some students will see part of the value of a degree as an opportunity to access areas of employment which might otherwise be closed off to them. The acquisition of a law degree (and subsequent qualification as a barrister or solicitor) has in the past been seen as a gateway to social mobility, although the extent to which academic success can outpace other factors such as class, familial connections and social

[28]Law Society, "SQE1 Functioning Legal Knowledge Assessment Specification" <www.sra.org.uk/sra/policy/sqe/sqe1-functioning-legal-knowledge-assessment-specification/> accessed 24 July 2020.

[29]Bob Hepple, "The Renewal of the Liberal Law Degree" (1996) 55 Cambridge Law Journal 470, 477.

[30]139 of the 164 respondees.

[31]90 of the 164 respondees. The most common theme was being generally interested in law or having enjoyed it at A-Level.

[32]Department for Education, "Reviewing Post-18 Education and Funding: Terms of Reference" (Department for Education 2018) <https://assets.publishing.service.gov.uk/government/uploads/system/uploads/attachment_data/file/682348/Post_18_review_-_ToR.pdf> accessed 21 July 2020.

[33]Alex Nicholson, "The Value of a Law Degree" (2020) 54 The Law Teacher 194.

capital is very much open to debate.[34] If our students want to become lawyers, want to earn money which allows them to repay debts or achieve other life objectives, what does this mean for those of us who teach criminal law and criminal procedure?

Against the background outlined above of consistent underfunding of criminal legal aid, fewer and fewer law students are progressing into practice as criminal solicitors or barristers. As fewer enter, the profession ages,[35] and low salaries in the sector combined with high debt levels have been highlighted by the Young Legal Aid Lawyers Group as posing a "significant barrier" to pursuing a career in legal aided areas of work.[36] In recent years, issues of wellbeing for practitioners have also come to the fore.[37] Many areas of concern focus on workload, underfunding, and the implications for work/life balance of inflexible court listings, which are likely to disproportionately affect criminal practitioners. Whilst students may well be attracted to criminal practice, does what we know of the economic prospects of such practice, the issues of wellbeing, and the social status of criminal practitioners within the profession have implications for how and what we teach? We will explore this predicament in the following section.

The ethics of teaching criminal law and criminal procedure

We recognise our relative privilege as legal academics. We are in secure employment within a sector that has undoubtedly some level of freedom. We recognise that this freedom is somewhat stifled by, inter alia, metrics such as the Research Excellence Framework and the Teaching Excellence Framework and – within law – changes to the degree in light of the Solicitors Qualifying Exam. Those of us working in higher education also face chronic problems such as precarity, pay gaps, pension poverty, and – as with criminal practice – increasingly unmanageable and unsustainable workloads.[38] Bearing in mind the factors surrounding our own employment and what we know of the criminal justice system, we find ourselves in an uncomfortable ethical position in respect of our students. During the module, "Crime, Law and Society" (initially devised by Newman and Harris, and on which we have all taught at various points over the past three years), we teach students about the problems with the criminal justice system and, in particular, the challenges faced by the criminal defence profession.

A number of these students express an interest in working within the criminal justice system, typically (although not exclusively) within criminal defence. Whilst the first half of the module engages students in debates regarding the demise of the criminal justice system and, in particular, the problems with – and faced by – the criminal defence profession, the second half exposes students to the practical realities – both positive and negative – of criminal practice. This part of the module introduces our students to many of the skills and experiences of criminal lawyers through a series of practice-facing sessions built around a fictional set of case papers. The two perspectives on the subject

[34] Sam Friedman and Daniel Laurison, *The Class Ceiling: Why It Pays to Be Privileged* (Policy Press 2019).

[35] Law Society, "Criminal Justice System in Crisis: Parliamentary Briefing" <https://tlsprdsitecore.azureedge.net/-/media/files/topics/criminal-justice/criminal-justice-system-in-crisis-briefing.pdf?rev=29f372a6c9a3448598f432807338e032&hash=D935AECA67833A38188D9DD8176D9D89> accessed 20 July 2020.

[36] Young Legal Aid Lawyers (n 15) 7.

[37] Richard Collier, "Anxiety and Junior Lawyers" in Alex Davies (ed), *Lawyer Health and Wellbeing: How the Legal Profession Is Tackling Stress and Creating Resiliency* (Ark Publishing 2020); Junior Lawyers Division, "Resilience and Wellbeing Survey 2019: Survey Report" (Law Society 2019).

[38] University and College Union, "Our Four Fights" <www.ucu.org.uk/media/10715/Our-four-fights/pdf/ucu_four-fights-explainer.pdf> accessed 28 July 2020.

area are presented by staff who bring different areas of academic and professional expertise; term one is taught by staff (Newman and Dehaghani) currently active in socio-legal research (with a focus on the criminal justice system) whilst term two is taught by a former criminal law practitioner (Harris). Through their reflective journals and through discussion with both module leaders, students are encouraged to reflect upon and communicate their developing and nuanced understanding of the problems facing the criminal defence profession and the criminal justice system more generally. This often results in an inherent conflict for our students: they have learned about the problems with criminal defence practice whilst also seeing how criminal defence can effectively contribute to enhancing the lives of others. Indeed, the module is in part designed to spark such reactions, having been initially born out of Harris' personal reflections upon the early days of training for the Bar and a pupillage in specialist criminal chambers in London after a horizon-widening year spent studying a Master's degree in Criminology.

For us, the challenges facing criminal defence (and the criminal justice system more broadly) raise an ethical dilemma in relation to those students who wish to pursue a career in criminal defence: without encouraging our students to enter the profession, we are in effect contributing to the demise of the profession; without "new blood", the profession is most certainly going to perish in 10–15 years' time, if not less. On the other hand, we feel reluctant to encourage our students to enter the criminal defence profession when we understand – through previous practice, through discussion with our colleagues and peers in the profession, and through our academic research and scholarship – that the profession offers few opportunities for social mobility and progression.

Part of the answer to how we address this question lies within the design of the module itself. The module is constructed, taught, and assessed in such a way that it surfaces these tensions and synergies for students and asks that they reflect upon them. This provides students with the space in which to recognise and acknowledge the conflicts they may feel. In recognition of our role as educators, we feel it important to critically reflect on our encouragement – or otherwise – of students entering the criminal defence profession. We cannot discourage our students from pursuing their passions but, equally, should we encourage our students to enter into a criminal defence profession when this profession – and the wider system within which it operates – is so evidently imperilled? We are still, then, left in a predicament about how to approach this tension. We thus challenge ourselves to work out what we can do to ensure that the profession has a future. It is to this matter that we turn in the following section.

Academia and institutional obligations

In seeking to understand these dynamics and impacts, Fineman's vulnerability theory is particularly illuminating. For Fineman, the state should "act to fulfil a well-defined responsibility to implement a comprehensive and just equality regime that ensures access and opportunity for all".[39] Not only can this be interpreted as a responsibility on the state to ensure that individuals can access justice through state-provided support, it can also be interpreted to include a state responsibility to ensure that graduates can access – so far as possible – career opportunities. In order to do so, however, there must be a viable career

[39] Martha A Fineman, "The Vulnerable Subject and the Responsive State" (2010) 60 Emory Law Journal 251, 273–74.

to enter into. Whilst essential to understanding human – or individual – vulnerability, Fineman's theory also urges us to consider the vulnerability of institutions:

> Institutions as well as individuals are vulnerable to both internal and external forces. They can be captured and corrupted. They can be damaged and outgrown. They can be compromised by legacies of practices, patterns of behavior and entrenched interests that were formed during periods of exclusion and discrimination, but are now invisible in a haze of lost history.[40]

Thus, institutions – such as a publicly funded criminal defence profession – can be vulnerable and compromised: in England and Wales, the criminal defence profession has been eroded and undermined by years of funding cuts and fee stagnations. However, these issues do not simply affect the profession itself and by extension those working within it. The problems cannot be severed from the ways in which they have an impact upon those who are studying law (particularly criminal law and procedure) and those who are teaching it. The exposed vulnerabilities may not stem simply from the demise of the criminal defence profession but certainly cannot be disconnected from it either. Vulnerability theory alerts us to the inescapable fact that "we are not atomised, separate beings; we are inter-connected".[41]

The demise of the institutions – and the dwindling numbers of jobs – mean that our students, when they graduate, will have fewer options available to them, or at least options that are feasible. Students who are saddled with large debts, particularly those from low income households and/or with little to no support system, may abandon their ambitions to earn money. The rightful reluctance on the part of our students to enter into the profession may call into question our role as educators. Whilst the value of a degree cannot be shaped or determined by career prospects, such considerations are nevertheless important. A vulnerability analysis highlights the interconnectedness of such problems: without encouraging our students to enter practice we may indirectly contribute to the (further) demise of the profession, and the absence of a profession may render our roles as criminal law and justice educators redundant. A vulnerability analysis highlights that we are not rational, liberal, autonomous beings as we think we may be, but we depend on institutions, relationships and networks, and these things, too, are dependent on us.

As such, students and their teachers cannot detach themselves from what is happening to the criminal defence profession: the crumbling of criminal defence has impacts upon teaching and learning, and whilst there is a place for teaching criminal law and procedure without a view to our students entering the profession, it may be more difficult to near impossible to sustain our teaching without drawing upon practice (whether in the form of input from practitioners and/or research with practitioners).[42] But there is a more fundamental issue at hand here: within a vulnerability analysis, do we as teachers and our institutions as educational (and public service) providers have a role to play in pushing back against further cuts and, by extension, limits to our students' prospects?

---

[40] Martha A Fineman, "The Vulnerable Subject: Anchoring Equality in the Human Condition" (2008) 20 Yale Journal of Law and Feminism 1, 18.

[41] Dehaghani and Newman (n 1) 1207.

[42] Of course, it could indeed be argued that criminal defence would still exist as a profession, albeit one that is not publicly funded. However, that line of reasoning falls short on at least two bases: first, that legal practice (and therefore criminal defence practice) is a public service and second, that without public funding, vast numbers of people would go unrepresented perhaps making the profession (if privately funded) obsolete.

It is therefore important that we, as academics and educators (and indeed as citizens), use our positions to expose the problems with the criminal justice process and the problems facing the criminal defence profession, whilst at the same time taking steps to support the profession.[43] However, with increasing workloads and increased precarity, this is not entirely possible, at least for us as individuals to achieve. As such, we believe that it is the duty of universities to engage with these questions and, in pursuance of their civic mission, to provide the time, space and resource to counter the problems faced by the criminal defence profession. Following Fineman, whilst institutions are themselves vulnerable (and such was exposed during Covid-19 with some universities facing financial hardship and, in some cases, bankruptcy),[44] they can also be a source of resilience. Universities, rather than being concerned with research and teaching metrics, could realise their value in supporting local communities in a real and meaningful manner; they could place their institutional gravitas behind their teaching and research staff (many of whom are working hard in the pursuance of social and criminal justice); they could cease competition with one another (recognising their mutual reliance) and instead put such energies into improving society for those who rely on social welfare (such as criminal legal aid).

Fineman's vulnerability theory alerts us to the interconnectedness of our existence: the problems facing the criminal defence profession are not simply problems for criminal defence practitioners to shoulder. They are problems that will inevitably affect many of our students and, by extension, are problems that we encounter in our teaching practices and need to bring into our classrooms. Recognising the position we occupy as academics – and some of us were formerly both law students and practitioners – gives us a sense of responsibility and a desire to help fight for something we believe to be important. We can see the role to be played by legal academics in working to preserve access to justice in the criminal sphere (and beyond). Yet, the institutions within which we work – i.e. the university or universities – must also commit to their civic mission agenda; the burden should not be for the individual to bear.

Conclusion

The module on which we teach together arose as a result of reflective conversations about our different experiences of and perspectives upon the criminal justice system and a shared desire to help students recognise the complex relationships between a theoretical examination of that system and practical participation within it. As educators and as reflective practitioners, especially in times of such rapid change both within the academe and beyond it, we find it is increasingly necessary to continue this process of reflection upon our position, being honest with students whilst also supporting them. The constant and iterative process of interrogating what we teach and why becomes more important to all of us.

Within this process, we are aware of problems in the criminal justice system and, in particular, the challenges faced by criminal practitioners. We feel a duty to play a role in fighting to protect an institution that we see great importance in. That said, the task of

---

[43]Fabrizia Serafim has called for the use of the concept of "extensão" – see F Serafim, [article].

[44]Camilla Turner, "Thirteen Universities Face Bankruptcy without Government Bailout, IFS Analysis Finds" *The Telegraph* (London, 6 July 2020) <www.telegraph.co.uk/news/2020/07/05/thirteen-universities-face-bankruptcy-without-government-bailout/> accessed 28 July 2020.

providing resilience to the criminal defence profession is not ours alone; universities should also play a greater role in supporting the legal profession. Doing so will not only illustrate that they take seriously their students' futures but that they also recognise – and place value on – contributing to wider society. This should not be born out of a concern for metrics, league tables, and neoliberal performance monitoring initiatives, but must emerge from a recognition of the university's role in wider society. The university has the ability and capacity for promoting social justice.

A vulnerability analysis allows for – indeed, demands – a recognition of the interconnectedness. It allows us to critically interrogate not only the dire state of criminal defence but also the ways in which individuals and institutions can undermine and support change. Doing so requires a reflexivity and a recognition of this interconnectedness. Vulnerability theory also allows us to mount a successful challenge to neoliberal ideology: it draws our attention to the ways in which neoliberal discourses present individuals and institutions as self-sufficient and autonomous, failing to expose the reliance on – and reliance of – individuals and institutions. This paper has aimed to highlight some of the many challenges in teaching criminal law and procedure in the face of a crumbling criminal justice system. It is not intended to provide all the answers to the crisis facing criminal justice or, indeed, the crisis facing universities. What we have sought to do is express some of the questions that we have asked ourselves as academics and, in so doing, we have explored some of the problems and possibilities in the hope of prompting further discussion and debate.

Vulnerability theory is central to this; it may have the potential to radically transform society and to radically transform the higher education landscape. We hope that ongoing dialogue on the role that legal academics could play, with regard to our students and the wider legal profession, will progress with an understanding of the insight that can be provided by taking vulnerability seriously.

Acknowledgements

We are incredibly grateful to Graham Ferris for providing the inspiration for this paper, and to Graham and Martha Albertson Fineman for their invitation to contribute to this special issue of *The Law Teacher*. We are also grateful to our students for their vital role in causing us to reflect on our teaching and research practices. All errors and omissions are our own.

Disclosure statement

No potential conflict of interest was reported by the authors.

Vulnerability theory as a tool against a banking model of legal education

Fabrizia Serafim

ABSTRACT

In this paper, I examine how university-based legal education has been facing pressures founded on a growing free-market fundamentalism which strengthen in law schools worldwide a model of education that Paulo Freire termed "banking". In countries of Latin American constitutionalism like Brazil, such pressures also entail the denigration of progressive understandings of the social right to education which have been inscribed in their constitutions. Against this trend, I contend that engaged law educators could benefit from using vulnerability theory, a critical legal theory devised by Martha Albertson Fineman, as a pedagogical tool considering how it lends itself to immediate use in the analysis of legal categories and in the problematisation of legal systems in a way not readily available to general critical pedagogies. In this way, legal educators can open up dialogues that promote awareness in law students who might otherwise resist discussing these topics because they are opposed to their expectations from law schools, aligned as they might be with market-based understandings of the purposes of a legal education.

Introduction

This paper originated from a presentation given at the "Vulnerability and the Organisation of Academic Labour Conference", hosted by Nottingham Law School in conjunction with Emory University, on Friday 25 and Saturday 26 October 2019 at Nottingham Trent University, UK. The workshop's call for papers invited those interested to reflect on the degradation of the resilience of university-based legal education caused by the commodification and marketisation of educational systems and consider how law schools and individual academics who are engaged with the reproduction of fairer societies should respond to such challenges.

When reading this call for papers, I couldn't avoid thinking back about my own formative experiences with popular legal education based on Paulo Freire's critical pedagogy when I was a law student at the Universidade Federal do Rio Grande do Norte (UFRN), an institution that is part of the public federal university network in Brazil. I had the opportunity to practise popular legal education while working towards my law degree in a federal public university because the social right to education as inscribed in the Brazilian Constitution of 1988 encompasses not only teaching and researching but also something called "extensão", that is, in the more progressive understanding of this term, a dialogue with local communities.

Not only must students from institutions like UFRN engage in these three modes of education – teaching, researching and "extensão" – in order to graduate from public federal universities as per the Constitution, but all professors and academics also should engage with all three as part of their professional obligations. This triad shows how the "Citizen Constitution", as the Brazilian Constitution of 1988 is nicknamed, did not intend to have public universities as institutions dedicated exclusively to the training of professionals with technical expertise. They were to also be radically democratic places for the production of critical thought grounded on the exchange of knowledge amidst pluralism and decentralisation of power circuits.

Thus, the motivation to think about the questions highlighted in the workshop's call for papers came from my personal lived experience and ongoing interest in this area. I believe that questions about the purposes of a state-funded higher education are more complex, relational, and compromised with the reproduction of a just society than we normally concede. Awareness of the responsibilities of both those receiving, as students, and those constructing, as professionals, this very education is being lost. This thinning out of the purposes of public higher education is not a phenomenon that is happening in isolation; it is situated in a larger dismantling of what pre-eminent Brazilian scientist, Dr Miguel Nicolelis, called "a great national heritage which is the federal university network" in Brazil[1] and the worldwide trend mentioned as the basis for the workshop.

The ideas presented in this essay benefited enormously from the specific methodology used in this event, which was called an "uncomfortable conversation". This innovative methodology can be placed within an ongoing movement towards the construction, implementation and dissemination of feminist methodologies in academia. It implements a collective approach based on conversation and shares similarities with perhaps the most famous feminist methodology, that of consciousness-raising. In discussing Fineman's innovation, Nancy E. Dowd provides us with a well-ordered explanation of the several, complex layers of "uncomfortable conversations":

> First is the embrace of intellectual diversity even when it reflects profound disagreement. Second is the insight that one can learn most from those with whom you most disagree. Third is that disagreement is framed as constructive difference; that is, even when there are strong differences and claims of inadequacy, insufficiency, or error, the conversation is not personal. Often the conversation is political, as differences in perspective translate into differences in strategy. The commonality in overall goals of commitment to equality and justice, however, hold together the participants in the room. Fourth, this is a method that operates from an understanding of acceptance and comfort in the intellectual space even as it encourages strong critique and discomfort.[2]

The remainder of the paper has been organised in the following way. First, I will expand upon the social right to education as inscribed in the Brazilian Constitution of 1988 and explain in more detail the key term "extensão" with the aim to describe the constitutional context into which the Brazilian federal public university network was inserted prior to the market-based pressures towards commodification and marketisation it more currently has faced. Then, I will discuss how these pressures are related to those

---

[1] Miguel Nicolelis, "O mundo está perplexo com o desmonte da educação no Brasil" (*Brasil de Fato*, 26 June 2019) <www.brasildefato.com.br/2019/06/26/miguel-nicolelis-o-mundo-esta-perplexo-com-o-desmonte-da-educacao-no-brasil> accessed 26 August 2020

[2] Nancy E Dowd, "The 'F' Factor: Fineman as Method and Substance" (2010) 59 ELJ 1191, 1198.

that several systems of higher education worldwide are having to confront and how they bring us back to what Paulo Freire described as a "banking model of education".[3]

Finally, I intend to discuss how engaged law educators who want to oppose such resilience-corrosive pressures could benefit from using vulnerability theory as a tool in their educational practices, considering the shortcomings of having at their disposal solely unspecific critical pedagogies, particularly that of Paulo Freire who focused mainly on education as liberation for the oppressed. By contrast, these professionals deal on a daily basis with those whom Freire deemed "the oppressors".[4]

1. The social right to education and the emancipatory notion of "extensão"

The Brazilian Federal Constitution of 1988 can be seen as part of an ongoing Latin American constitutionalism,[5] enshrined in its original text and then altered through the many constitutional amendments that have added a somewhat long list of fundamental rights of a social nature. After decades of public, dogmatic and jurisprudential debates, these rights are now widely understood to be on a par with political rights. These social rights are structured by a juridical system that, among other characteristics, allows for their judicial enforcement as individual or collective subjective rights. They serve as objective parameters against which the (un)constitutionality of law passed by the legislative power and normative acts enacted by the executive power can be evaluated.[6]

Among these social rights is the right to education (Brazilian Federal Constitution, Article 6). The social right to education is inscribed in the constitutional text as a right for all and the duty of the state, as well as the family, which must be promoted and fostered with the cooperation of society so it is not limited to the delivering of capable workers but explicitly encompasses the full development of the person and their readiness for the exercise of citizenship in a plural, democratic society (Brazilian Federal Constitution, Article 205). Not shying away from discussing the role higher education should play in this endeavour, the Constitution of 1988 also declares that universities shall have autonomy in didactic, scientific, administrative, financial and property management matters as well as comply with the principle of non-dissociation between teaching, research and extension.[7]

I will expand on this interesting principle below, but before that it is important to have in mind the shape of the social right to education in general and how it relates to university-based higher education. In particular how Brazilian constitutionalism is an open, ongoing

---

[3]Paulo Freire, *Pedagogy of the Oppressed* (Continuum Publishing 2005).

[4]ibid.

[5]Latin American constitutionalism has been described as a practical and theoretical effort to enable liberation from colonialism, that is, a social and political situation of unjust domination, oppression, and exploration of the region by economically developed countries in the Global North and as an alternative to liberal, elitist constitutionalism. Antonio Carlos Wolkmer and Samuel Mânica Radaelli, "Refundación de La Teoría Constitucional Latinoamericana: pluralidad y descolonización" (2017) 37(II) Derechos y Libertades <https://e-archivo.uc3m.es/bitstream/handle/10016/27134/DyL-2017-37-wolkmer.pdf>

[6]It would be impossible to go into much detail about the topic in this paper. For more on Latin American constitutionalism, see Antonio Carlos Wolkmer and Oscar Correas, *Crítica Jurídica na América Latina* (CENEJUS 2013); Boaventura de Sousa Santos, "Refundación del Estado en América Latina: perspectivas desde una epistemología del Sur" (Instituto Internacional de Derecho y Sociedade 2010). For more on social rights in the Brazilian Constitution of 1988 see Claudia Toledo, *Direitos Sociais em Debate* (FGV 2013); Ingo Sarlet, "Os Direitos Sociais a Prestações em Tempo de Crise" (2014) 15(2) EJJL <https://portalperiodicos.unoesc.edu.br/espacojuridico/article/view/6876>

[7]Constituição da República Federativa do Brasil (1988).

project that depends on how courts, specially the country's constitutional court (Supremo Tribunal Federal), interpret it. So far, the jurisprudence appears to point towards an understanding of the social right to education that comprehends the importance of addressing structural problems and recognises the state's responsibility in creating and mediating between different social actors involved with the provision of education.

Two cases illustrate this point. In one of them, judged by Justice Sepúlveda Pertence, the constitutional court has decided that public universities in Brazil are one example of the few instances in which the constitution has mandated the exercise of direct democracy through popular participation.[8] Moreover, in a case that dealt with a programme that established positive actions based on race, ethnicity, and income in higher education, the court affirmed that steps towards promoting universal access to higher levels of education did not interfere with the economic freedom of private universities. In this case, Justice Ayres Britto concluded that:

> The connection of all the constitutional devices hitherto cited, highlights the realization that education, especially school or formal education, is a social right that everyone must attain. For this reason, it is the duty of the State and one of its public policies of the highest priority.[9]

With these points about the social right to education in mind, it becomes possible to expand upon the before-mentioned principle of non-dissociation between teaching, research and "extensão" inscribed in the Brazilian Constitution of 1988 and to focus on the groundbreaking aspects of the last part of this triad. In concentrating on this specific point, I am circumscribing a long road of discussions and disputes that have been and – as the next topic of the paper shows – still are being made about the meanings and purposes of education in general and of university-based higher education in particular.

More commonly, "extensão" means outreach events which Reis called *eventista-inorgânica extensão*.[10] These are "assistencialistic" practices, that is, practices that dehumanise people because the practice treats them as docile and passive recipients of state benefits or of charity donations while depoliticising the institutional arrangements that are in place to (not) meet human needs. Freire described "assistencialism" as policies of financial, technological or social assistance which attack symptoms, but not causes, of social ills and that do not promote awareness about the possibility of changing said institutional arrangements nor facilitate the creation of political democratic spaces where it would be possible for communities to reflect on and make decisions about the structural causes of their social realities.[11]

But "extensão" in a more progressive and innovative sense is an innovative attempt to produce emancipatory knowledge and social change in the universities involving their students and professionals, in accordance with the constitutionally mandated radical democratic underpinnings of these social institutions, as well as society at large. It is interesting to note that Paulo Freire wrote about a very similar topic, that is, the extension of agricultural knowledge from technical schools to peasants.[12] The educator explained that he would rather have this dialogical process of knowledge

---

[8]Ação Direta de Inconstitucionalidade número 244/1992. Brasil. Supremo Tribunal Federal. Relator Ministro Sepúlveda Pertence.

[9]Ação Direta de Inconstitucionalidade 3330/2012. Brasil (Supremo Tribunal Federal. Relator Ministro Joaquim Barbosa 2012) 18.

[10]Renato Hilário dos Reis, "Histórico, tipologias e proposições sobre extensão universitária no Brasil" (1996) 2 LC <https://doi.org/10.26512/lc.v2i2.2610>

[11]Paulo Freire, *Extensão ou Comunicação?* (Paz e Terra 1983) 128.

[12]ibid.

production called "communication" in an attempt to distance exchanges from inclinations towards assistencialism that practices of "extensão" might assume.

In doing this, the progressive notion of "extensão" demands that universities are responsible for the formation of critical subjects and participant citizens, and it therefore delegitimises any restriction of the role of the university to the production of a qualified workforce according to market demands only. Also, this notion moves beyond what the specialised literature has called colonial power-knowledge circuits that are marked by rigid dichotomies in which emotions must be separated from reason, lived experiences have no say, and only controlled experiments are valid.[13] It rejects the paradigm in which one group of people is the object of study while another group is the only one capable of doing research and the teachers impart knowledge that has to be absorbed without the active participation of the students. Finally, understanding "extensão" in such a way, and making it indissociable from teaching and research, facilitates the creation of public discourse about how technologies and scientific knowledge are developed and applied – discourse that exists in tension with a focus on the benefit of the private economic powers that historically have been financing both these ventures.[14]

This progressive and emancipatory understanding of "extensão" and, in turn, of the purposes of higher education and the responsibilities of the professionals and institutions that compose the Brazilian federal university network is indebted to Paulo Freire's critical pedagogy. In this sense, both the research and the teaching missions of the university are affected by it. Understood not as outreach events that bring down assistance from the university to destitute communities, but as an open dialogue between different social actors that together construct knowledge and reflect upon the social conditions that make that reality be what it is, "extensão" is a practice that works against what the famous Brazilian educator has described as a banking model of education.

With the term "banking", Freire intended to describe a model of education that treats students as passive objects that receive and not as active subjects who construct knowledge. A banking model of education focuses on ensuring that technical knowledge is passed down instead of also having as one of its aims the "conscientização" of the students, that is, in very broad terms, fostering the capacity to think critically about social reality and not to assume it is natural and immutable.

2. Attacks on the social right to education – a move back towards a banking model

As mentioned before, the workshop from which this paper originated was held in order to gather individuals interested in reflecting about how university-based legal education has been facing pressures founded on neoliberal free-market fundamentalism.

Sociologist Christian Laval has discussed precisely how education is increasingly treated as a commodity. He shows how neoliberal ideology has advanced towards school systems worldwide but beginning from the United States, imprinting in them neoliberal values. To an increasing extent, schools are to be guided by principles such as

[13]Walter D Mignolo, "Prophets Facing Sidewise: The Geopolitics of Knowledge and the Colonial Difference" (2005) 19 Social Epistemology 111.

[14]For more on the subject see Joel Samoff and Bidemi Carrol, "Influence – Direct, Indirect and Negotiated: The World Bank and Higher Education in Africa" in Guy Neave, *Knowledge, Power and Dissent* (UNESCO 2006). See also Sandra Harding, *Objectivity and Diversity: Another Logic of Scientific Research* (University of Chicago Press 2015).

"innovation" and "efficiency"; respond to market demands; be measured by economic indicators, and ranked like companies. They are not to waste time in the formation of participant citizens and individuals capable of critical thought.[15]

Kelsey notes this worrisome trend in regard specifically to higher education:

> There was no place in this agenda for the nation-building function of universities; no virtue in an educated population of graduates and academics committed to the society which invested in them; no inherent value in education and knowledge if it was not highly rewarded in the current commercial market; no purpose in academic contributions to research, policy, legislation, and public debate; no need for expert analysis and public critique which was free from party-political and commercial vested interest.[16]

On the Brazilian system of a public federal universities network, these pressures follow a worrisome trend that, although reaching unprecedented levels with the far-right government now in power, did not start with the current administration. For example: there were measures that supplanted university and academic independence and the provision of resources as ways to ensure the quality of education was supplanted by criteria that resemble new social control tools. These tools are already in use in other areas of public life and serve to measure positive performance leading to competitiveness among professionals employed in the public sector and to enforce constant output from them. They were put in place during the administrations of the Brazilian Worker's Party (Partido dos Trabalhadores). Also, during their administrations, mechanisms (PROUNI, FIES) were adopted to publicly fund students enrolled in private institutions thus providing public money to strengthen private institutions and as a consequence diverting money from the public system of higher education.[17]

This complicates a narrative in which there are easily identifiable good political groups that are always knowledgeable about and in favour of the general good, as well as equally easily identifiable bad guys. Current far-right governments must be understood in the context of their historical development and not seen as a surprise attack that apparently came from nowhere.[18] After all, market-based reasoning is pervasive and capable of moulding political actors traditionally situated on the left. Observing that such trends started with centre-left governments might lead one to conclude that it is important for critical legal theory to try to grasp overarching ideological assumptions and properly address how institutions are created and perpetuated by law. In the Brazilian case, an entire constitutionally inscribed public system of higher education based on a social right to education is affected by such ideology and reasoning.

However, the reforms that have been recently proposed by far-right governments are also more markedly pushing forward the defunding of higher education and for its privatisation, justified by free-market fundamentalism. The most concrete example is the federal government proposed programme for universities, "Future-se", which contends that more entrepreneurship and less public funding are good outcomes for Brazilian universities and

[15]Christian Laval, *A Escola Não É Uma Empresa* (Boitempo 2019).

[16]Jane Kelsey, "Privatizing the Universities" (1998) 25 JLS 63 <https://www.jstor.org/stable/1410455?seq=1>

[17]Cristina Helena Almeida de Carvalho, "O PROUNI no governo Lula e o jogo político em torno do acesso ao ensino superior" (2006) Educação e Socidade <https://doi.org/10.1590/S0101-73302006000300016> accessed 29 August 2020. Also R Guimarães-Iosif and AV Santos, "The Contradictions of Corporate Governance in Brazilian Higher Education" in L Shultz and M Viczko (eds), *Assembling and Governing the Higher Education Institution* (Palgrave Studies in Global Citizenship Education and Democracy. Palgrave Macmillan 2016) <https://doi.org/10.1057/978-1-137-52261-0_17> accessed 29 August 2020.

[18]Sabrina Fernandes, *Sintomas mórbidos: a encruzilhada da esquerda brasileira* (Autonomia Literária 2019).

their professionals.[19] The programme also focuses on science, technology and mathematics, thus conveying the message that critical thought closer to social sciences and the humanities is a deviance from higher education's legitimate purpose.[20]

João Carlos Salles, rector of the Universidade Federal da Bahia and current president of Andifes (Associação Nacional dos Dirigentes das Instituições Federais de Ensino Superior), correctly asserted in an open letter through which he explained his personal reasons to oppose that this university complied with this federal programme, that the government had the intention of transforming the entire structure of the federal public higher education through the adoption of a particular and unconstitutional vision of what are the purposes of the Brazilian public federal network of universities.[21]

3. Vulnerability theory as a tool against a banking model of legal education

Facing such pressures, legal academics and other professionals look for pedagogical tools that might help them to oppose such trends in their daily practices. Among them is Paulo Freire's critical pedagogy. He was a rather prolific writer who discussed many different topics within the general realm of critical pedagogy. Many of his insights are important to guide engaged professionals immersed in the task of teaching in law schools worldwide in resisting the "banking model" of education which, as discussed in the previous section, is a contemporary pressure higher education faces. Nonetheless, Freire's critical pedagogy is not a panacea.

At least two difficulties arise when thinking about how to apply Freire's method to law schools. First, his writings originated from his practical work engaged in the process of teaching impoverished adults, who for structural reasons did not attend school when young, how to read and write. Therefore, to the best of my knowledge, there is no stepped Freirean method developed specifically to be used within university-based legal education that is readily available to these professionals who are already overworked with bureaucratic and productivity demands.

Second, his method is primarily intended to be used with a part of the population that has not benefited from the structures and institutions that have benefited the "oppressors" (to use Freire's terminology), a category that would include legal professionals. Nor is his method devised to be used with a part of the population that will largely go on to compose the very social institutions, that is, the judicial and legislative powers, that are markedly known for their respective roles in perpetuating the status quo.

In a book revealingly called *Para uma Revolução Democrática da Justiça* (Towards a Democratic Revolution of Justice), Boaventura de Sousa Santos discussed possible ways to cross the bridge between Freire's critical pedagogy and university-based legal education.[22] He discusses how the formation of judges and the legal culture at large is an essential part of any imagined institutional change in the judiciary's power. To this

---

[19]More information about this governmental programme can be found on its website: <http://portal.mec.gov.br/component/tags/tag/52641)> accessed 27 August 2020.

[20]For more comments on this recent trend in Brazil, see Fernando Cássio (ed), *Educação contra a barbárie: Por escolas democráticas e pela liberdade de ensinar* (Boitempo 2019).

[21]The open letter can be found at <https://ufba.br/ufba_em_pauta/por-que-o-conselho-universitario-rejeitou-o-future-se> accessed 29 August 2020.

[22]Boaventura de Souza Santos, *Para uma revolução democrática da Justiça* (3rd edn, Cortez 2011).

end, Santos defends the necessity of a revolution in law schools, which are marked by the banking model of education. Such a revolutionary change would aim not simply to fall into a technical or dogmatic perpetuation of legal knowledge, but to engage law students in sociological analysis, which would in turn make these students more context-sensitive. Santos calls this method creating an "ecology of juridical knowledge" to pit against a "monoculture of scientific knowledge".[23] The method not only aggregates different technical-scientific disciplines, like sociology and philosophy, but also recognises the importance of promoting a dialogue between different knowledges and founts of law, derived as they are from a myriad of worldviews, practices, and modes to understand humans themselves, as well as the relationship between humans and nature.

It is hard to disagree with Boaventura's analysis – law schools are increasingly replicating a model that can be described as a banking model of education. Those invested in the attainment of fairer societal arrangements must engage in creative ways to change this predicament, keeping in mind the importance of education in opening up dialogues that promote awareness of the social realities in which we are immersed.

Although Santos' preferred method to achieve this, that is, the creation of an "ecology of knowledge", is necessary, it is not sufficient. Legal education needs to go through the elaboration and employment of critical *legal* theories in teaching practices. More importantly, it must incorporate a critical legal theory that confronts the overall ideological assumptions that are hidden in legal systems and traditional curricula.[24]

I defend this importance of using specifically focused critical legal theories that problematise the ideology that underpins modern legal systems for a pragmatic reason that is based on experience in legal popular education. The hardest part in employing a critical perspective in law schools was not engaging with the so-called "general population" or the "popular masses", but engaging with those who were in the process of gaining a legal education.

Fellow students were reluctant to engage in any of the diverse theories that can fit under a broad understanding of critical theories – ranging from Frankfurt School to feminism, critical race theories, Foucaldian studies or post/de-colonial theories – since they did not directly relate to their training or expertise in law. Law students were inclined to see such reflections as something that other university-based courses would better explore or something that was only of interest to postgraduate researchers politically inclined to the left.

While they were mistaken in not realising the value of a more humanist education in law schools for democratic republics that hope to follow a constitutionally inscribed rule of law,[25] the students were not wrong to point out that analysing legal institutes and categories is what those trained in law can do best. They felt that in doing this task, they fulfilled their responsibilities towards society. However, the question they should have asked was why not do precisely that but in a way that raises critical consciousness regarding the ideological assumptions that legitimate current legal systems and uses of law, particularly neoliberal understandings of privatised liberty, responsibility and ownership?

---

[23] ibid 99.

[24] Alexandre Pereira Hubert, "O Currículo Oculto como uma Forma de Análise da Reprodução Social e Cultural na Faculdade de Direito" in Antonio Carlos Wolkmer and Oscar Correas (eds), *Crítica Jurídica na América Latina* (CENEJUS 2013).

[25] The first article of the Brazilian Constitution states: "The Federative Republic of Brazil, formed by the indissoluble union of the states and municipalities and of the federal district, is a legal democratic state."

It is in this scenario that I see vulnerability theory as a tool readily available to those who are teaching law in ways that a more general critical pedagogy – like Paulo Freire's – or critical theories are not. Vulnerability theory, as distinctively elaborated by Professor Martha Albertson Fineman[26] and continually developed by academics related to the Vulnerability and Human Condition Initiative,[27] offers the vulnerable legal subject the opportunity to dislodge the (neo)liberal legal subject that has oriented law and policy in Western, liberal, capitalist democracies. By problematising the legal subject and situating it in the historical context of neoliberalism, a vulnerability approach makes it possible to identify the "autonomy myths" that justify the (neo)liberal legal subject and open up the possibility to ponder whether what exists now could (or should) be otherwise. Thus, vulnerability theory helps move critical theories in general beyond the segregation of society into different minority categories and helps us to think in terms of institutional arrangements and ideologies that underpin everything and everyone.[28]

That in itself is already a big achievement in relation to university-based legal education because those who are immersed in it normally do not pause to ponder in mandatory courses offered in law schools what are the assumptions that precede legal categories and institutions that are being taught along with the juridical practice most students are bound to be involved with in the near future. But vulnerability theory does not stop there. This critical legal theory starts with the legal subject and goes on to study how one or other version of it structures our understanding of what is an appropriate state response to human needs – what is an appropriate shape social institutions might take if they were to ethically respond to the human condition which is not one of abstract invulnerability but one of social embeddedness and biological embodiment.

In this sense, one practical use of vulnerability theory in law school classrooms could be to address the unfortunately common question for "a casual student of international economic law": "how the framework relates to capitalism".[29] This question could be tackled with a (perhaps long and most likely received with rolling eyes by students) lecture about how different Marxist traditions have approached the question of law. Or with a discussion of how one particular social hierarchy might or might not relate to or be constituted and perpetuated through law. By using vulnerability theory, a legal educator facing such a question could start by thinking seriously about core values of international economic law (or of liberal law at large) itself and how they organise (or do not organise) through law the responsibilities that should address the material lived reality of universal human vulnerability.

Another use could be for exploring how vulnerability theory isolates, problematises and promotes critical consciousness towards the principle or value of equality, an overarching category that legitimises modern Western legal theory and legal systems. Through the years a formal conception of equality that ends up equalising differences and erasing what

---

[26]For an overview of the theory see Martha Albertson Fineman, "Vulnerability and Inevitable Inequality" (2017) 4 Oslo Law Review 133 <https://ssrn.com/abstract=3087441> accessed 31 August 2020. For a discussion of the application of vulnerability theory see Martha Albertson Fineman, "Reasoning from the Body: Universal Vulnerability and Social Justice" in Chris Dietz, Mitchell Travis and Michael Thomson (eds), *A Jurisprudence of the Body* (Palgrave Socio-Legal Studies, Palgrave Macmillan 2020).

[27]For more information about the initiative see <https://web.gs.emory.edu/vulnerability/> accessed 16 February 2021.

[28]Thomas Piketty, *Capital and Ideology* (Harvard University Press 2020).

[29]This observation was made by Mohsen al Attar in a book review. Mohsen Attar, "Pathology or Plutocracy? The Misery of International Law" [2019] *Leiden Journal of International Law* <https://doi.org/10.1017/S0922156519000463> accessed 16 February 2021.

Fineman has called "inevitable inequalities"[30] is taking hold in mainstream legal academia and juridical practice. The prominence of this notion of equality can be noted in the many discrimination laws enacted and related academic writing published.

Vulnerability theory does not dismiss the continued importance of formal equality mandates to address socially constructed hierarchies in individual instances and on a more fundamental level shares the modern value that all humans are morally worth the same. But it does highlight how such an approach is insufficient to understand and regulate through law relations where differing levels of authority and power are inevitable. Examples of inevitable inequalities regulated through law are the legal category of parental authority, which regulates the relationship between child and parent, and the working contract, which regulates the relationship between employee and employer. Only when these inevitable inequalities are brought to light in legal theory does it become possible to discuss asymmetrical responsibilities that must be differently allocated if fairer social outcomes are to be achieved.

Coming back to critical pedagogy, it is interesting to note that Freire's critical pedagogy has since the 1970s alerted us to the inherent difference between those who teach and those who are being educated and how the former have particular responsibilities towards the latter. In this light, both Freire's critical pedagogy and Fineman's critical legal theory alert us to the dangers of a simplistic understanding of equality. Recognising that there are inequalities that are essential to the functioning of human societies like the one between teacher and student or between parent and child makes it possible to perceive and discuss what are the responsibilities that arise from these inequalities. And it is in this discussion of responsibilities not of individuals but of social categories ("teacher"/"parent") and of social institutions ("school"/"family"), which are constructed through state law that the path towards an understanding of our collective responsibilities (that is, the responsibilities inherent in these categories and also of institutions, states, international organisations) is opened up.

In sum, because vulnerability theory is a *legal* theory, it is a more readily available tool in the task of crossing the bridge from teaching with "the oppressed" to teaching with "the oppressors" (to again use Freire's terminology) or those who perhaps inadvertently, perhaps uncritically help in the maintenance of structures – more precisely, of institutions and categories created by laws, that benefit some to the detriment of others. And it does so in a straightforward way, that is, by questioning the very subject of rights – a concept that every law student learns in their first years of professional training – and not by asking reluctant students to deal with, sadly, still contested themes in society at large. Equally importantly, vulnerability theory lends itself to immediate use in the analysis of legal categories in such a way that in order to employ it one would not need to advocate a complete revolution in the curricula employed in law schools, nor have to face initial resistance from students in specific classes compromised with the general ideological framework.

Conclusion

In this paper, I have tried to articulate reasons according to which vulnerability theory, a critical legal theory and a theory of justice first devised by Martha A. Fineman and

[30]Fineman, "Vulnerability and Inevitable Inequality" <https://www.idunn.no/oslo_law_review/2017/03/vulnerability_and_inevitable_inequality> accessed 16 February 2021.

continuously being developed by both her work and that of scholars worldwide associated with the Vulnerability and Human Condition Initiative, can be a useful tool at the disposal of engaged professionals who teach in law schools. I bring it into conversation with what Paulo Freire, Brazilian educator and philosopher who famously pioneered works on critical pedagogy, termed a "banking model of education".

This model of education is ever more pervasive in law schools worldwide given the pressures university-based legal education has been facing because of a growing free-market fundamentalism. In Brazil, I see this trend as opposing emancipatory understandings of the social right to education which include more progressive understandings of the practice of "extensão", part of a triad that, alongside teaching and researching, should guide higher education in the country – and perhaps in other countries as well – according to a constitutional mandate.

That is because vulnerability theory shares premises similar to both Freire's critical pedagogy and "extensão", notably the objective of achieving fairer societies through the building of emancipatory institutional arrangements and their focus on the responsibilities of educational professionals in bringing about awareness of and critical stances towards uncovering free-market fundamentalisms which are trotted out as "normal" and "inevitable" in our societies. To adapt some of Freire's critical pedagogy terminology, the awareness that vulnerability theory encourages in law students is a valuable way for opening up debates about unfair social realities with the "oppressors" and thus enacting a higher educational system of liberation. This would also make it more probable that these students engage in practices of "extensão" that do not mean assistencialistic events, but hold space for dialogue with the wider community and for reflection with them about what are the responsibilities of legal systems and universities in the reproduction of unjust social hierarchies and institutional arrangements.

More specifically, vulnerability theory is more useful in law classrooms than a general critical pedagogy because it deals directly with legal categories and the myths that underpin them, categories that also permeate mainstream legal academia and the technical preparation for judicial practice. This critical legal theory lends itself to immediate use in the analysis of legal categories. In order to employ it one would not need to advocate a revolution in law schools or a curriculum overhaul – not even for a specific discipline. Vulnerability theory can be used by any professor, lecturer, or tutor in any traditional law course in such a way that it relates directly to the immediate interests of law students.

Disclosure statement

No potential conflict of interest was reported by the author.

Funding

This study was financed in part by the Coordenação de Aperfeiçoamento de Pessoal de Nível Superior – Brasil (CAPES) – Finance Code 001.

The positive and negative roles of grant funding as mechanisms for societal transformation and the development of community resilience

M. Joan Wilson and W.R. Sexson

ABSTRACT

Grant funding sought by academics for research or service activities can facilitate societal transformation and the development of community resilience. Grant funding, for the purpose of this paper, will refer to funding from govern- mental sources. Funding can be an agent for transformation and resilience for individuals and communities but has both positive and negative consequences. Previous work has failed to address why, even when a grant provides funding for the development of measures with seemingly positive impact, those measures may not be accepted or sustained, or may be perceived in a negative way by the community they are meant to benefit. We have found that the key to maintaining the positive effects (and potential resilience) of any community-focused grant-funded activity is to engage the community during proposal development in goal setting and activity planning, and in the dissemination of the research or programme findings. These measures aid in community acceptance of the grant objective and enhance the sustainability of the outcome, thus having a positive impact on resilience. Involving the community in early planning and throughout the process enhances capacity and facilitates stronger relationships between the academic grantee and the community that can potentially allow for further transformative activities.

Introduction

Socio-legal or clinically informed legal research generates ethical issues around the relationships forged, or relied upon, in the course of the research. The problems may be raised by the power of the elite participants in some cases or by the powerlessness of participants who individually and as a community lack resilience.[1] Some legal research falls between these two stools, being concerned

[1] In the first class is research reported in such works as: Alan Paterson, *Final Judgment: The Last Law Lords and the Supreme Court* (Hart Publishing 2014); Richard Moorhead, Steven Vaughan and Cristina Godinho, *In-House Lawyers' Ethics: Institutional Logics, Legal Risk and the Tournament of Influence* (Hart Publishing 2018). In the second class is research reported in such works as: Mary McClymont and Stephen Golub (eds), *Many Roads to Justice: The Law-Related Work of Ford Foundation Grantees Around the World* (Ford Foundation 2000); Liz Curran "A Research and Evaluation Report for the Bendigo Health–Justice Partnership: A Partnership between Loddon Campaspe Community Legal Centre and Bendigo Community Health Services" (2016) <http://lcclc.org.au/wp-content/uploads/2017/11/HJP-full-and-final-report.pdf> accessed 16 September 2020.

with those state officials and professionals who mediate between ordinary people and the state.[2] Research into access to justice and unmet legal need seeks to understand the experience of people and to argue for legal reform in their name.[3] Finally, there is a body of research into cause lawyers, lawyers whose legal careers are devoted to social justice or support for social and political causes.[4] In all these situations research or practice ethics need to go beyond compliance with institutional proprieties and engage with the relationship between the researcher or clinician and the community or communities she seeks to serve. In this area legal researchers can learn lessons from the experience of medical researchers.

A key career-development pathway for the academic professional is through grant-funded research, particularly funding from governmental sources that provides multi-year salary support and indirect costs to the institution; it is often a required element to sustain an academic career. Obtaining a grant and completing the grant-related deliverables builds sustainability and thus resilience of academic institutions by increasing the potential for future funding and research. Research and grant-funded programmes can also be transformative in that they build capacity and resilience in communities that are the subject of the research. Because many community members do not understand the essence of academic research or the grant-associated funding mechanisms, this research can also have an adverse impact on the community perceptions and may cause the researcher and/or academic institution to be viewed negatively by community partners. We illustrate these points in the context of grant-funded research conducted on the social determinants of health[5] in low-resourced, economically disadvantaged communities in metropolitan Atlanta. Failure to adequately address these negative perceptions can result in a loss in existential resilience of the researcher/academic institution and result in the failure of academic–community collaboration. This collaborative failure results in gaps in current knowledge, decreases in grant-funded service delivery and potential rejection of future offers of grant-funded collaboration for the academic researcher. Furthermore, it can also result in the failure to build the trust necessary to reinforce resilience in the targeted communities.

For many of the (US) governmental agencies that provide funding to address the various social determinants of health, the term "vulnerable" is commonly used to define the populations that are the target of the research. There are a number of definitions of the term "vulnerable populations", but in general, the term is used in medicine and public health research to describe a sub-segment of the community where inequality of resources is present or where special consideration and protections in research are needed.[6] While the

---

[2]An example being: Roxanna Dehaghani, *Vulnerability in Police Custody: Police Decision-Making and the Appropriate Adult Safeguard* (Routledge 2019).

[3]Hazel Genn, *Paths to Justice: What People Do and Think about Going to Law* (Hart Publishing 1999); The Legal Services Board and The Law Society, "Legal Needs of Individuals in England and Wales Technical Report 2019/20" <www.legalservicesboard.org.uk/wp-content/uploads/2020/01/Legal-Needs-of-Individuals-Technical-Report-Final-January-2020.pdf> accessed 16 September 2020.

[4]Austin Sarat and Stuart Scheingold (eds), *Cause Lawyering: Political Commitments and Professional Responsibilities* (Oxford University Press 1998); Kieran McEvoy, "Cause Lawyers, Political Violence, and Professionalism in Conflict" (2019) 46 Journal of Law and Society 529.

[5]The World Health Organization (WHO) defines the social determinants of health as "the conditions in which people are born, grow, live, work and age. These circumstances are shaped by the distribution of money, power and resources at global, national and local levels." <https://www.who.int/health-topics/social-determinants-of-health#tab=tab_1> accessed 17 March 2021

[6]Preethi Shivayogi, "Vulnerable Population and Methods for Their Safeguard" (2013) 4(1) Perspect Clin Res 53.

term "vulnerable populations" is used to describe a variety of socially, educationally or economically disadvantaged groups within society, our work refers particularly to marginalised and economically disadvantaged ethnic minorities. There is considerable research relating to "vulnerable populations" focusing on groups such as children, pregnant women, prisoners, or physically and intellectually challenged individuals and the legal regulations that govern research with these sub-segments of the population.[7] There is however, a gap in the research in addressing why, even when a grant provides funding for seemingly positive measures, those measures may not be accepted – or worse, may possibly be perceived negatively by the community that the measures are meant to benefit.

Fineman recognises vulnerability as the "fundamental reality of the human condition",[8] and describes "the human condition as one of universal and continuous vulnerability".[9] As was previously stated, in the medical and public health realm, the term "vulnerable populations" is commonly used in reference to certain subgroups of the population, and is used as a basis of comparison, in that some people are perceived as more or less vulnerable than others.[10] Fineman asserts that designating populations as "vulnerable" causes a stigmatising effect, implying victimhood or negative connotations. She has detached the concept of vulnerability from specific subgroups and uses the term to define what it means to be human.[11] We are all vulnerable by virtue of the fact that we are human, but we have different levels of resilience, which is at the heart of Fineman's vulnerability theory. While all human beings experience vulnerability, we are positioned uniquely to deal with it due to differences in our embodiment and due to our embedded differences in social institutions and relationships.[12] Resilience is the way in which vulnerability can be mitigated, both for the researcher and for the research subjects.

The Belmont Report, created as a result of the National Research Act of 1974, identified the ethical principles that should undergird any research involving humans. The three principles put forth by the Act have become the basis for the ethical approach to patient-involved research and clinical care and are: (1) respect for persons, (2) beneficence (doing good/avoiding harm), and (3) justice.[13] The Report states that involving "vulnerable subjects" (including but not limited to racial minorities and the economically disadvantaged) may denote a "special instance of injustice", due to their ready availability, dependent status, administrative convenience or the ease of manipulating them due to their socioeconomic condition.[14]

It is a common perception in many low-resourced communities that academic institutions receive *large sums of money* through grant awards, which they use to pay salaries to researchers to come into their communities to do research. There is also a perception that little of this money actually goes to community members for participating in the research. The academic researchers utilise the services of community members as part of focus groups and other data collection activities, and the community members are paid what is often considered a marginal stipend (or a low-value retail gift

---

[7]These regulations include such measures as protection of rights, well-being, safety, privacy and confidentiality of vulnerable subjects (ibid).

[8]Martha Albertson Fineman, "Vulnerability and Inevitable Inequality" (2017) 4 Oslo Law Review 133.

[9]ibid 134.

[10]ibid 142.

[11]Martha Albertson Fineman, "The Vulnerable Subject and the Responsive State" (2010) 60 Emory Law Journal 251, 266.

[12]See Fineman (n 8) 143–45.

[13]Office of the Secretary, National Commission for the Protection of Human Subjects of Biomedical & Behavioral Research, "The Belmont Report" (18 April 1979).

[14]ibid C.3.

card) for their time. Other common complaints are that as soon as the funding period is over, the researchers leave and there is no dissemination of the study findings to the community. The community and its residents perceive little or no benefit from the project. The project or programme funded by the grant ends, and there is no funding (or public will) to sustain it. The researchers move on to new studies, and thus new pools of grant funding, and the community is left with the same inequities and problems that existed before the grant was obtained. The Council for International Organizations of Medical Sciences (CIOMS) has stated that "vulnerable populations", that is those individuals and groups addressed by the research, have the same entitlements to access the possible benefits of research as the rest of the population,[15] but that often does not occur. Complicating these issues is general distrust, especially in African-American communities in the United States, of dubious or unethical research stemming from incidents such as the Tuskegee Syphilis Study.[16] All of these factors create challenges for researchers conducting studies in low-resourced communities.

Partnering with communities to conduct research addressing the fundamental social issues that they experience is important for closing the knowledge gap, yet it is difficult for communities or community organisations to unilaterally obtain significant government funding. From a community perspective, they are precluded from applying for research grants that are only offered to academic institutions. It is often necessary to provide "evidence base" in order to justify the funding, and community members do not have the prior research data to support this – even though the community was the subject of prior research grants. Individuals in the community most often do not have the knowledge or resources to apply for grants, to collect and analyse data, to monitor and evaluate the study, or to disseminate the study findings – activities that are required by many funding agencies. They also do not have the capacity to be a fiscal agent for large awards and produce the deliverables such as financial and programmatic reporting that are often required. Community organisations and community members do, however, have the front-line, grassroots expertise and know the issues better than most academic researchers could possibly understand, so their input and collaboration are vital to the integrity of the study.

Community-based participatory research

Just as the Belmont Report described ethical principles to protect the rights and well-being of research participants, the concept of community-based participatory research (CBPR) seeks to provide a framework to protect the rights and well-being of communities. CBPR is a model in which the research process is intended to benefit research participants and the communities in which they live.[17] While research has been conducted in communities for many years, it is only in more recent years that the focus has shifted to CBPR. CBPR involves more than the activity of research being conducted in a community. The Agency for Healthcare Research and Quality (AHRQ) defines CBPR as "a collaborative

[15]Council for International Organizations of Medical Sciences (CIOMS), *International Ethical Guidelines for Biomedical Research Involving Human Subjects* (CIOMS 2002) 41.

[16]Dwayne T Brandon, Lydia A Isaac and Thomas A LaVeist, "The Legacy of Tuskegee and Trust in Medical Care: Is Tuskegee Responsible for Race Differences in Mistrust of Medical Care?" (2005) 97 Journal of the National Medical Association 951.

[17]Daniel S Blumenthal, "Is Community-Based Participatory Research Possible?" (2011) 40 American Journal of Preventive Medicine 386.

research approach that is designed to ensure and establish structures for participation by communities affected by the issue being studied, representatives of organisations, and researchers in all aspects of the research process to improve health and well-being through taking action, including social change".[18] In CBPR, the research team, academic institution, and the community all play active and equitable roles in each phase of the research.

It is critically important for the research team to involve members and leaders of communities in determining the research focus and to do so within the early planning stages of research design – to not do so risks gaps in the evidence with the funded programmes not meeting the true needs of the community. This includes the participation of representatives from the community in each project phase – research design, budget development, programme planning, implementation, data collection, monitoring and evaluation and dissemination of results. By so doing, many potential barriers can be addressed and possibly mitigated. In removing barriers, research becomes more accepted by the community and the potential for better community acceptance of research outcomes enhances the resilience associated with the research.

Researchers have reported persistent barriers in attempting to involve people from low-resourced communities in research and challenges for academics working in communities. One of the major barriers to collaboration, and an issue that creates friction between researchers and the community, is inadequate compensation for community members. Involving them from the planning stages allows both parties to negotiate a fair compensation for their time and effort, and to budget for this compensation in the grant proposal. Other barriers include transportation and childcare during research activities such as interviews, surveys or focus groups. Because of these barriers, retention of community members in research studies is often challenging. Providing those services (or adequate compensation to cover the cost and time) helps to ensure the cooperation and participation of community members.

Other challenges revolve around a general mistrust of research and researchers, and a perception of hidden motives. Often, researchers who are not familiar with the community will use language, context and perspective that differs from that of the community. Community members in low-resourced communities may have inadequate reading and/or comprehension skills to fully understand the extent of their involvement. Removing barriers to research participation, for example by using simple language or illustrative pictures where literacy is an issue or having a stronger focus on project design with community collaboration will help to alleviate some of the difficulty and sensitivity of doing research in low-resource communities and will allow researchers to better fill knowledge gaps for these populations.

Risks and unintended consequences of research

Researchers in low-resource communities have reported risks associated with their community research such as dealing with community members with perceived aggressive or threatening mental health issues or aggressive dogs. When the community is unwelcoming to academic research, this can pose risks for the researcher, and police are

[18]M Viswanathan and others, "Community-Based Participatory Research: Assessing the Evidence: Summary" (2004) Aug (99) in *AHRQ Evidence Report Summaries* (Agency for Healthcare Research and Quality (US) 1998–2005) <www.ncbi.nlm.nih.gov/books/NBK37289/#A148901> accessed 17 March 2021

often not called in low-resourced communities due to distrust. Emory University's Urban Health Initiative, a programme of the School of Medicine, does a considerable amount of grant-funded research in low-resourced communities, and has developed a "Safety and Wellness" course for its researchers, staff and volunteers to help them to be aware of the potential risks, both seen and unseen, that they could potentially encounter while working in communities.[19]

Other challenges are associated with reimbursements to community members for their time or expenses. Often, because of university finance procedures, the community members must spend money first, then submit for reimbursement. While this is routinely done by university employees, it can be difficult for community members with limited computer and/or internet access to scan and email receipts. Also, many cannot afford to wait for reimbursement or may not have bank accounts for Automated Clearing House (ACH)[20] online deposits, which is required by some universities for payment. There are similar issues for stipend payments. Paperwork and technology are often required. Many low-income community members do not have bank accounts, and universities often do not permit cash payments.

Many researchers fail to realise the potential for unintended consequences of their research. One recent example involved a research project that required the testing for the build-up of lead and other heavy metals in blood samples from children in Atlanta Georgia's Westside community.[21] The houses in the community were all built prior to the ban on lead paints in the United States in 1978. Over time, a significant amount of the lead-based paint peeled off the houses and fell to the ground where the children played. Additionally, a vacant field in the same community was a former slag dumping area where the heavy metal by-products of a foundry were disposed. The research into the levels of lead and other toxins was important to the well-being of current and future children in the community.[22] Although this is an important public health project that had the potential to expose a toxic environmental issue that could affect the neurological development of children, many of the community residents were very ambivalent about this project. For many residents of this community, their main (and for some, their only) asset was their home. This study happened around the time of a major redevelopment of the area, in which developers and investors aggressively approached the community residents to try to purchase their homes for a development project that many in the community referred to as "gentrification". Documentation of toxic levels of heavy metals on their property could have a detrimental effect on the only potentially

---

[19]The Emory Urban Health Initiative's (UHI) self-paced Safety & Wellness course contains content promoting safety during the heightened climate around social reform, racial equity, and the current Covid-19 pandemic. The Safety Manual included with the course provides guidance on practices during advocacy activities that promote safer, equitable communities, and tips on how to maintain Covid-19 safety in the midst of reopenings and increasing political demands. The course is open to students, faculty, staff, local professionals, and community members at <https://emory.instructure.com/courses/43718> accessed 17 March 2021.

[20]Automated clearing house (ACH), an electronic funds-transfer system used commonly in the US to facilitate payments.

[21]This research was a collaboration between Emory University and members of the Atlanta Westside community, which led to a site investigation by the US Environmental Protection Agency (EPA). For more information, see: Candis M Hunter and others, "Perspectives on Heavy Metal Soil Testing Among Community Gardeners in the United States: A Mixed Methods Approach" (2019) 16 International Journal of Environmental Research and Public Health 2350.

[22]Lead poisoning can occur from the gradual build-up of lead in the body over months or years. Lead poisoning can cause serious health problems, particularly in children, where it can lead to serious physical and mental disease including developmental delay, hearing loss and seizures. See <www.mayoclinic.org/diseases-conditions/lead-poisoning/symptoms-causes/syc-20354717> accessed 17 March 2021.

significant financial opportunity that had come their way in a very long time. Many felt that finding out about levels of lead in their soil might not help them if they could not afford to do anything about it, and the knowledge of this would devastate their property values.[23] Parenthetically, it is of interest that the lead levels in the soil were likely high for a long period of time, but coincidentally, it was only when financial development appeared likely that soil sampling was done.

Adverse childhood experiences (ACEs) and mental health issues

Other unintended consequences of doing research in low-resourced communities can occur when the research evokes post-traumatic responses related to prior adverse experiences (i.e. adverse childhood experiences or ACEs). The personal safety and emotional support of the community members needs to be considered prior to the start of the study if the study is capable of producing emotional trauma.

Recommendations

There are a number of positive outcomes that can potentially result from collaboratively engaging the low-resourced community in academic grant-funded research. By utilising some of the specific strategies mentioned below, it is possible to increase the knowledge and skills of community members, thus having a positive impact on their resilience. Including community members in all phases of the project design, implementation, and dissemination of findings will help to build trust and facilitate community buy-in of the project, and may have a positive impact on the scientific value of the research.

Changing institutional practices that currently inhibit CBPR, such as modifying institutional processes to streamline payments to community members and earmarking university funds to support CBPR would better enable community participation. Other strategies that universities could employ include mentoring faculty and students on CBPR, modifying tenure and promotion guidelines to promote CBPR, using Institutional Review Boards (IRBs) to promote CBPR, and making CBPR-oriented faculty appointments.[24]

Some of the ways that grant-funded research in communities can build capacity and promote resilience in communities include:

- Providing training to community members to supplement data collection. Having data collected by community members can foster trust in the community. It also provides training that may aid those community members in employment opportunities. Pay them a living wage for their work.
- Develop a community steering committee and offer stipends to participants for their time and expertise.
- Provide stipends or compensation to community members for referring their friends and family members to the study.

[23]The authors do not mean to imply that public health research such as this should not be done if it could lead to adverse economic consequences, but consideration should be given in advance to what type of adverse consequences might occur, and how to mitigate them.

[24]Philip Nyden, "Academic Incentives for Faculty Participation in Community-Based Participatory Research" (2003) 18 J Gen Intern Med 576.

- Include community members as co-authors in publications, or co-presenters at local and national conferences. Also, assist them in authoring or presenting on their own – help them to be able to tell their own story and to become viewed as "experts" in their field. Assist them with opportunities for speaking engagements for a respectable amount of money.
- Involve the community members in all phases of the project, including grant writing and budget development. The research consortium should include community members as key persons in grant writing, data collection, and paper writing so that the key community members begin to build the knowledge and résumé components necessary to become credible in their own right.
- Include community members in leadership roles for the project.
- Help community members to pass their General Educational Development (GED) tests[25] and other educational offerings.
- Develop internships, certificates and other educational offerings for community members to help to build their résumés.
- Develop a safety manual for students and volunteers (both in the community and in the academic institution) who will be working with the grant-funded project/programme.[26]

With the engagement of the community on the front end on goal setting, activity planning, and dissemination of research findings or programme outcomes, the community is more likely to positively engage with the research team and produce sustainable results at the conclusion of the grant funding, thus having a positive impact on resilience.

Conclusion

Fineman has noted that "A vulnerability approach argues that the state must be responsive to the realities of human vulnerability and its corollary, social dependency."[27] One mechanism currently used for fulfilling this state responsibility (albeit only incompletely) is through the funding and approval of grants. Looking at this topic through the lens of vulnerability theory, it is important to consider the inequality of resilience. The measurement of equality of circumstances is predicated on comparison of individuals or groups considered equals. Because of a past history of discrimination and overtly unequal treatment codified in law, this approach generates concerns of treatment differences, unequal approaches and hidden agendas. It follows that grant programmes, where governmental grant money is targeted at an intermediary (e.g. a university department) generate suspicion and unequal treatment in the community which is supposed to be the recipient of positive benefit of the grant programme.

Social and academic institutions can use grant-funded programmes and research as a way to bring about positive change in the communities of their target populations by building resilience to counter vulnerability. Likewise, the researcher needs existential resilience to persevere in the face of challenges and obstacles in his/her research. Resilience can be strengthened in the communities through human capital assets,

---

[25]General Educational Development tests are a group of subject tests which when passed, provide certification of high school level academic equivalency in the US and Canada. The GED is considered an alternative to a high school diploma for those who did not complete secondary school.

[26]See n 15.

[27]Fineman (n 8) 134.

such as those provided through education and training. Resilience is enhanced when academic researchers convert our community research "subjects" into our research "partners". In return for their unique perspectives and insights, we provide them with opportunities for new knowledge and skills. Resilience for both the community and the academic researchers can be strengthened by a focus on removing current research and grant-related barriers to participation by the community members, resulting in better sampling and data collection and greater buy-in by the community.

The context for academic research and grant writing must be changed. Academic researchers should not approach research participants for grant-funded research by considering them "vulnerable populations" (thus focusing on their deficits). Rather the focus of grants and community-based participatory research should be on building resilience in the individual as well as in the targeted communities. In this way, the researcher and academic institution, as well as the funding agency, are acting as a responsive state in their capacity for providing mechanisms for building resilience in the community. The result of this shift would help to build resilience in the academic research team/institution as well.

These lessons apply across the disciplines of law and medicine. The problems that have been documented in the interactions between cause lawyers and the social movements they try to serve illustrate this.[28] In a UK academic setting the approach discussed above could be conceptualised in terms of impact and evaluation of research interventions.[29] However, the lessons transcend local audit cultures and disciplinary conventions, and speak to the essential values of social justice research and the informing of a responsive state.

The shift from category-based or individual autonomy-based vulnerability to Fineman's model of universal vulnerability requires an accessible and inclusive research design, and for all parties – the researchers, academic institutions, and funders – to consider the relationships between these partners in a different way. Recasting the way we think of the communities in which we do research would put us on the path to better science in terms of validity and merit, and allow us to leverage a more responsive state that ensures better opportunity and resilience for all.

Disclosure statement

The authors have no relevant financial or non-financial competing interests to declare in relation to this paper.

[28]Austin Sarat and Stuart A Scheingold (eds), *Cause Lawyers and Social Movements* (Stanford University Press 2006).

[29]Richard Watermeyer, *Competitive Accountability in Academic Life: The Struggle for Social Impact and Public Legitimacy* (Edward Elgar 2019); Liz Curran and Pamela Taylor-Barnett, "Evaluating Projects in Multifaceted and Marginalised Communities: The Need for Mixed Approaches" (2019) 19 Evaluation Journal of Australasia 22.

The university's fragile role in fostering societal resilience by facilitating the development of community-engaged professionalism

W.R. Sexson and M. Joan Wilson

ABSTRACT

The university plays an essential role in the education and social development of professionals. This role is vulnerable in that state support is required to foster sustainability and resilience, especially as the university goes about its job of assuring community-focused professionals. Vulnerability theory and its correlate, resilience, offer a lens to look at the university's responsibility to train professionals who act in the best interest of the community. In the past decades, "professional identity formation" has been a primary focus of medical education. Professional training in key "core competencies" demand development of the character traits, commitments, and skills that are essential to the appropriate knowledge, ethical behaviours, social awareness, and community focus necessary for the engaged healthcare professional. The Covid-19 pandemic has placed previously unconsidered stressors on the university and in doing so, has unmasked a variety of system-generated vulnerabilities. As the university attempts to remain solvent, it has responded so as to decrease the ability of the academic professional to engage in social justice activities. This paper addresses universities' social justice commitment to their academic (professional) faculty and makes recommendations that Universities might undertake to support their own community-focused commitments.

Introduction

In October 2019, the Vulnerability and the Human Condition Initiative held an international, invited workshop in collaboration with Emory University, Nottingham Trent University and the University of Leeds. The title of the workshop was "Vulnerability and the Organisation of Academic Labour". The speakers and authors at the conference included academic and other professionals from a variety of schools and positions representing universities both in the United States and across the United Kingdom. The focus of the conference was to survey academic labour using vulnerability theory, resilience change strategies and professionalism in looking at university-related teaching and training in the professions.

As a result of these presentations and discussions over three days in Nottingham, England, a number of the discussants were invited to collaborate in producing a journal issue dedicated to the outcome of the deliberations. This is one of those papers.

The professions, professionalism and social justice

This article is an attempt to "take professionalism seriously" in a very specific way, by holding professional bodies to their public service ideals.[1] Professional ethics generally purport to hold professionals to standards that go beyond economic self-interest,[2] and we argue that engaging students with these aspects of professional ethics should be an integral part of any professional education.[3] While our focus is on medical ethics because this body of knowledge is our area of expertise, the lessons learned can become models for legal professional ethics. Indeed these lessons may become collaborative models that affect society in a truly collaborative fashion. Our focus is on the most general commitments to the public good, and thus the approach taken here avoids the false dichotomy between teaching the professional code and ignoring professional ethics as an inherently technical aspect of a training model of professional education.[4] The commitment to justice expressly articulated in medical ethics may be only implicit in some systems of legal ethics and where this is so a comparison with medical ethics might prove salutary.[5] If we intend to take the aspirational commitments of professional ethics seriously then we need to embed them in professional education, including legal education.

Society gives a number of privileges and responsibilities to professions (e.g. self-regulation, autonomy, respect) and to the professional.[6] In exchange, these professions and their members have reciprocal obligations (integrity, social responsibility, truth-telling, etc.),[7] both implicit and explicit, to engage positively with the people and community in which the professional lives and works. This societal engagement and the consequent potential for positive transformation are key parts of the way that the professional provides value to society. This discussion draws heavily on our perspective

---

[1]Richard L Abel, "Taking Professionalism Seriously" [1989] Annual Survey of American Law 41. Significantly, this was a paper given at a conference devoted to the social responsibility of the lawyer. As we will see below restrictive practices go back to the dawn of medical ethics, although our focus is on the quid pro quo of public service.

[2]Edmund D Pellegrino, "Character, Virtue and Self-Interest in the Ethics of the Professions" (1989) 5 Journal of Contemporary Health Law & Policy 53.

[3]Thus, this article is another attempt to address the problem of how to teach professional ethics in an engaging and relevant manner, see: William H Simon, "The Trouble with Legal Ethics" (1991) 41 Journal of Legal Education 65. It is also an attempt to respond constructively to recommendation 7 of the LETR: Julian Webb and others, "Setting Standards: The Future of Legal Services Education and Training Regulation in England and Wales" (Legal Education and Training Review 2013) 287–88.

[4]In the UK a conflict between a "vocational" and a "liberal" legal education has been a powerful and persistent conceptual frame for considering legal education, and especially undergraduate law, see: William Twining, *Blackstone's Tower: The English Law School* (Sweet & Maxwell 1994) 52; Fiona Cownie, "Introduction" in Fiona Cownie (ed), *Stakeholders in the Law School* (Hart Publishing 2010) 2–4. In the USA a similar bifurcation has been articulated as a dispute over the purpose of legal education – whether it should serve the profession or the academy, see: Harry T Edwards, "The Growing Disjunction between Legal Education and the Legal Profession" (1992) 91 Michigan Law Review 34; Richard A Posner, "The Judiciary and the Academy: A Fraught Relationship" (2010) 29 University of Queensland Law Journal 13.

[5]The Solicitors Regulation Authority sets out as its first principle of conduct: "You act in a way that upholds the constitutional principle of the rule of law, and the proper administration of justice" <www.sra.org.uk/solicitors/standards-regulations/principles/>accessed 17 September 2020.

[6]Anne Bertkau, Jaclyn Halpern and Sanjay Yadla, "The Privileges and Demands of Professional Self-Regulation" (2005) 7 Virtual Mentor 267.

[7]Catherine Thomasson, "Physicians' Social Responsibility" (2014) 16 Virtual Mentor 753.

as healthcare professionals. However, the principles of professionalism, societal advocacy and social justice are not unique to the healthcare arena.

It is the role of the university not only to teach professionalism, but to partner with the student professional in developing their professional identity. This combination of training and professional identity formation is an essential part of the university's commitment back to society by training the professional to confront vulnerability and enhance resilience. Society's reciprocal response to the professions is to allow wide latitude and professional say in function, certification and importantly rewards (e.g. financial, social status and positive regard).

The professions and their members (professionals) have the implicit obligation to positively engage and transform the communities in which they live and work. The professional has an inward-facing, workplace responsibility internal to their dealings with their patient, client and customer in the context of the issue for which the person is contacting the professional. Virtually every professional grouping and most universities support social justice and positive social engagement as a fundamental professional responsibility. In contrast to the inward-facing client/patient focused responsibility, this social responsibility is an outward-facing commitment to foster social justice.

In terms of social justice and vulnerability theory, the commitment of the university and the academic professional is to be responsive to human vulnerability and social dependency. The term the authors have used since about 2014 for this professionalism-related social responsibility is "engaged professionalism". This term denotes the professional who, with the proper motivation, ethic and training, acts to enhance social opportunity and resilience in both individuals and communities.

Vulnerability theory and the university

Vulnerability theory, as developed by Professor Martha Albertson Fineman, argues that the state and its social institutions (e.g. universities, professional societies, organised groups, etc.) have the responsibility to respond to the realities of human vulnerability by facilitating resilience individually and socially.[8] Fineman's view of vulnerability and resilience stems from Feminist Legal Theory. As part of this theory Fineman contends that there is a myth surrounding the popular notion of individual independence and autonomy.[9] In traditional legal theory, governments and social institutions, because of this presumed autonomy, have little responsibility for fixing these individual problems. Fineman posits that it is this approach to the mythical autonomous individual that actually promotes discrimination and stigmatisation by placing some people into "vulnerable groups" in order to focus special attention and particular remedies on them. Alternatively, Fineman argues that vulnerability should be viewed as universal and constant – an inherent part of the human condition.[10] It is resilience, both individual and societal, that mediates and mitigates the vulnerability. The state and various social entities (e.g. the university, professional societies) are responsible for the broad implementation of resilience within society. In this conception, the inevitable vulnerability can be either embodied (that is vulnerability within the individual) or embedded (vulnerability because the individual

[8] Martha Albertson Fineman, "Vulnerability and Inevitable Inequality" (2017) 4 Oslo Law Review 133.
[9] Martha Albertson Fineman, *The Autonomy Myth: A Theory of Dependency* (New Press 2004 xxiv) 387.
[10] Martha Albertson Fineman and Anna Grear (eds), *Vulnerability: Reflections on a New Ethical Foundation for Law and Politics* (Gender in Law, Culture, and Society series, Ashgate 2013).

exists within institutions). Thus, it is not only persons but our social institutions that are inevitably vulnerable.[11] It is the unmasking and recognition of latent, albeit inevitable, vulnerability that then engenders a response from the individual or the institution. The facilitation of the response to inevitable and universal vulnerability, that is resilience, may arise singularly from the individual and their own resources or reserves, or it may be mediated by the government, by various social institutions or by socially conscious actors, e.g. professional societies and the professional. In professional legal and medical training, generally at a university, the focus of effort is on the acquisition of knowledge, skills and behaviours of the professional. Thus the facilitation and mentored tutelage in this advocacy role of the professional may be thought of as less important or overlooked completely.

Not only are individuals vulnerable, but entities and institutions are also universally vulnerable. As vulnerable entities, the university, professional organisations, and by extension the academic and the professional, may be confronted with stressors that challenge their very existence. While universities are so large that they may not be considered as significantly vulnerable, external threats may unmask the vulnerability inevitably present. Such threats include poor academic reviews, decreases in funding of grants (especially those with sizable indirect reimbursements), decreased state funding, uninspired economic development, poor endowment management and downturn in the economic market which threatens the value of the investments making up the endowment – or even a pandemic, as discussed below. As the university recognises its vulnerability, it regains institutional homoeostasis by trying to regain its prior vitality. This is accomplished by a number of administrative and economic ploys which have the downstream effect of unmasking the vulnerability of faculty, staff, employees and the students. Thus vulnerability theory extends to the organisation of academic labour, the topic of the October 2019 Nottingham conference.

The university and the development of the professional

The university plays a number of key roles in society and in relationship to the professional. The university is responsible in part for training the professional; for being one of the repositories of professional knowledge; for the organisation and implementation of professional programmes related to the inward-facing and outward-facing responsibilities of professionalism (see above). Academic professionals are the ones creating new knowledge and are the conduit for the accomplishment of programmes promoting social justice. In this context, it is the university and its professionals that develop, organise and implement new approaches to social as well as personal resilience.

In the health-related schools the general concept of the university's mission is that of the metaphorical three-legged stool. The "legs" supporting the stool are the commitments to education, research and clinical pursuits. It is on these three legs that the health institution's mission, functions and goals rest. Interestingly, although social justice and advocacy are generally thought to be part of the university's mission and are stated in many schools' mission statements, these roles are understated in comparison to the other roles. Thus, even when mentioned, advocacy and attention to social justice become only a vestigial fourth leg of this academic stool. Many faculty members whose primary focus is on advocacy or social justice may find it difficult to get

[11] ibid 3.

promoted. Similarly, because of the separation of one training programme from another (e.g. Otolaryngology from Internal Medicine or Neonatology from Neurosurgery) social justice training is even less homogenously addressed.

The student professional, as an immediate part of their training, is made clearly and poignantly aware of their obligation to the professions and their social obligations. Very shortly after arrival at school, the student is brought into a solemn "white coat ceremony". As part of the ceremony, the student is charged with their obligation to patients and to society, they frequently recite the Oath of Hippocrates and are finally given their first white coat. As the white coat is put on, the student is reminded that the simple wearing of the coat sets them apart from the rest of society and confers with its wearing the obligations of the profession, to people and to society.

Hippocrates (circa 400 BCE) wrote one of the earliest and longest-lasting codes of ethics in existence. The code is noted by Heubel to be the "soul of professionalism".[12] In this context, the Hippocratic Oath is the basis not only for medicine's contract with society, but for all similar professions and their own societal contracts. The oath follows as cited here:

> I swear by Apollo the physician, and Aesculapius, and Health, and All-heal, and all the gods and goddesses, that, according to my ability and judgment, I will keep this Oath and this stipulation – to reckon him who taught me this Art equally dear to me as my parents, to share my substance with him, and relieve his necessities if required; to look upon his offspring in the same footing as my own brothers, and to teach them this Art, if they shall wish to learn it, without fee or stipulation; and that by precept, lecture, and every other mode of instruction, I will impart a knowledge of the Art to my own sons, and those of my teachers, and to disciples bound by a stipulation and oath according to the law of medicine, but to none others.
>
> I will follow that system of regimen which, according to my ability and judgment, I consider for the benefit of my patients, and abstain from whatever is deleterious and mischievous. I will give no deadly medicine to any one if asked, nor suggest any such counsel; and in like manner I will not give to a woman a pessary to produce abortion. With purity and with holiness I will pass my life and practice my Art. I will not cut persons laboring under the stone, but will leave this to be done by men who are practitioners of this work. Into whatever houses I enter, I will go into them for the benefit of the sick, and will abstain from every voluntary act of mischief and corruption; and, further from the seduction of females or males, of freemen and slaves. Whatever, in connection with my professional practice or not, in connection with it, I see or hear, in the life of men, which ought not to be spoken of abroad, I will not divulge, as reckoning that all such should be kept secret. While I continue to keep this Oath unviolated, may it be granted to me to enjoy life and the practice of the art, respected by all men, in all times! But should I trespass and violate this Oath, may the reverse be my lot!

The oath is comprised of two parts. The first pledges the allegiance of the physician-to-be to the profession and to those who practise medicine. The physician is to treat those who "taught me this Art" as parents and to look upon other practitioners as family. The second portion of the oath deals with the commitments to the patient, and to society – and notably to self. The core duties of medical ethics today can be seen in the oath.[13] Commitments of the oath include those to beneficence, that is respect for persons; to avoid harm (non-maleficence); to confidentiality; to self-regulation; to personal and societal integrity; to veracity; to knowing personal limitations and to professional outreach (a form of social justice). Versions of this oath, whether in its entirety or as a

[12] Friedrich Heubel, "The 'Soul of Professionalism' in the Hippocratic Oath and Today" (2015) 18 Med Health Care Philos 185.

[13] Thomas L Beauchamp and James F Childress, *Principles of Biomedical Ethics* (8th edn, Oxford University Press 2019).

shorter, modernised version, are administered to virtually every student of healthcare in the United States and many or most students around the world. As a consequence of this commitment to the patient and to society, medicine and related professions (e.g. nursing, pharmacy, public health) along with law and theology are some of the few professions that have been granted special status by society.

In 2002, the American Board of Internal Medicine and the European Federation of Internal Medicine authored and published simultaneously "Medical Professionalism in the New Millennium: A Physician Charter".[14] The Charter was intended to articulate the fundamental principles of healthcare as well as a number of professional commitments intended for use not only by physicians, but by all healthcare professionals. The commitments of professionalism outlined in the Charter are noted to be the basis of "medicine's contract with society". The Charter has been ratified or adopted by over 140 professional organisations worldwide representing scores of millions of healthcare providers.

The three core principles of the Charter are ones that could be adapted for use by virtually any professional organisation. These general and foundational principles of professionalism include the following (with the accompanying explanations from the published charter).

Principle of primacy of patient welfare. This principle is based on a dedication to serving the interest of the patient. Altruism contributes to the trust that is central to the physician–patient relationship. Market forces, societal pressures, and administrative exigencies must not compromise this principle.

> *Principle of patient autonomy.* Physicians must have respect for patient autonomy. Physicians must be honest with their patients and empower them to make informed decisions about their treatment. Patients' decisions about their care must be paramount, as long as those decisions are in keeping with ethical practice and do not lead to demands for inappropriate care.

> *Principle of social justice.* The medical profession must promote justice in the health care system, including the fair distribution of health care resources. Physicians should work actively to eliminate discrimination in health care, whether based on race, gender, socioeconomic status, ethnicity, religion, or any other social category.

Accompanying the principles, the Charter sets out a number of professional responsibilities. These responsibilities are broad commitments to the profession, to the patient and to society such that any professional organisation could use them. Of special use while considering each of these responsibilities, enumerated below, is the description, not included here, with references and discussion that make the scope of the responsibilities useful in daily life. These commitments are:

> 1. Commitment to professional competence; 2. Commitment to honesty with patients; 3. Commitment to patient confidentiality; 4. Commitment to maintaining appropriate relations with patients; 5. Commitment to improving quality of care; 6. Commitment to improving access to care; 7. Commitment to a just distribution of finite resources; 8. Commitment to scientific knowledge; 9. Commitment to maintaining trust by managing conflicts of interest; 10. Commitment to professional responsibilities.

Training in professionalism generally occurs in the initial years of schooling. The term "professional identity formation"[15] has been used recently to describe the training

---

[14]"Medical Professionalism in the New Millennium: A Physician Charter" (2002) 100 Obstet Gynecol 170; "Medical Professionalism in the New Millennium: A Physician Charter" (2002) 359(9305) Lancet 520.

[15]Mark Holden and others, "Professional Identity Formation in Medical Education: The Convergence of Multiple Domains" (2012) 24 HEC Forum 245.

process of becoming a functioning member of a profession. In this formative process, the student and her/his mentors focus on the roles and responsibilities of the professional as she/he interacts with the patient, client, or customer in the context of expectations, work accomplished and payment relationships.

Professional identity formation is a relatively new concept in teaching of the healthcare professional. The concept includes teaching and experience in ethics as well as mentored psychosocial and behavioural training and supervision. The term is used to focus on the broad areas of personal, social and professional training used to bring the developing healthcare professional into a vigorous awareness of the commitments and demands of healthcare and the caring professions.

Goldie notes that the nature of identity formation is primarily social and relational.[16] Helping students to integrate the principles and commitments of their chosen profession into their "multiple identities" is fundamental to professional education. The principles and commitments of the Charter are used in forming curricula in most healthcare training institutions as well as many professional organisations. Professional identity formation is discussed as an integrative process which involves having the developing professional establish the values, moral principles and self-awareness that are part of psychological ego development and which are essential to social interaction.[17] This development is implicit to the developing professional and is ultimately essential to the transition of the professional from the classroom to interactive societal situations. The goal of the process is to ensure that the practising professional possesses an identity which embodies the value systems of the profession,[18] in support of patient professional commitments and interactions.

Cruess and others[19] importantly state that the journey from layperson to skilled professional is affected not only by "who they are", but by "who they wish to become".

The schematics discussed in this article make clear that socialisation, supported by role models, conscious reflection and experience are formative in the development of a robust professional identity. One of the questions for consideration at this conference is to evaluate the purpose and value of legal/professional education. Based on the literature on professional identity formation, the educational journey to become a professional must necessarily encompass didactic, experiential, and importantly, an internalised and reflective evolution of the self. With the inculcation of these factors, professionals can contribute significantly to the development of resilience in the individuals and communities in which she or he works.

The Accreditation Committee on Graduate Medical Education (ACGME) is the entity within the United States that defines the common requirements for all graduate medical education programmes nationwide (i.e. residencies and fellowships programmes).[20] ACGME oversight takes on the structured review of such things as sponsoring institutions, site review, personnel job descriptions, trainee eligibility requirements, faculty qualifications, the learning environment, curricular components, and evaluation. Of special

---

[16]John Goldie, "The Formation of Professional Identity in Medical Students: Considerations for Educators" (2012) 34 Med Teach e641.

[17]ibid (12).

[18]Richard L Cruess and others, "Reframing Medical Education to Support Professional Identity Formation" (2014) 89 Acad Med 1446.

[19]Richard L Cruess and others, "A Schematic Representation of the Professional Identity Formation and Socialization of Medical Students and Residents: A Guide for Medical Educators" (2015) 90 Acad Med 718.

[20]Elizabeth A Rider and Ruth H Nawotnaik, *A Practical Guide to Teaching and Assessing the ACGME Core Competencies* (2nd edn, HCPro 2010) 394; ACGME Common Program Requirements (Residency) (2018).

importance is the set of core competencies which provide the conceptual and training framework for the student physician professional.

The core competencies felt to be foundational to medical education include professionalism, patient care and procedural skills, medical knowledge, practice-based learning, interpersonal and communication skills and systems-based practice. Within the first of the core competencies, professionalism[21] the learner must demonstrate the following core professional behaviours: compassion, integrity, and respect for others; responsiveness to patient needs that supersedes self-interest; respect for patient privacy and autonomy; accountability to patients, society, and the profession; respect and responsiveness to diverse patient populations, including but not limited to diversity in gender, age, culture, race, religion, disabilities, national origin, socioeconomic status, and sexual orientation; ability to recognise and develop a plan for one's own personal and professional well-being; and appropriately disclosing and addressing conflict or duality of interest. These competencies in the context of professionalism and the professional identity are the outline for professional training not only in medical school, but through the rest of the professional's career.

The ACGME further states that programmes and trainees must understand the social setting (specifically the social determinants of health) from which the patients come.[22] Medical training programmes are required to fashion training content that is consistent with the needs of the community. The ACGME specifically states, in the intent section of item II.A.4.a, the following:[23]

> The mission of institutions participating in graduate medical education is to improve the health of the public. Each community has health needs that vary based upon location and demographics. Programs must understand the social determinants of health of the populations they serve and incorporate them in the design and implementation of the program curriculum, with the ultimate goal of addressing these needs and health disparities.

The ACGME, through its core competencies, prescribes attention to the health (well-being) of the public. This definitive charge within medical education provides focus and clarity to training programmes: "trainee professionals must be attentive to the needs and unique problems of the patients they serve".[24] Evaluating specific communities and service areas for resilience scarcity falls within the frame of vulnerability theory. The "engaged professional" may contribute to developing resilience within the defined deficiencies of the community based on the skills, values and compassion of the individual.

The university as a vulnerable entity

As stated earlier, individuals are vulnerable. They depend on the state and social institutions within the state (e.g. the family, the market, the educational system, etc.).[25] This dependence is reinforced in the laws and regulations of the state so as to identify need and to promote resiliency. These solutions according to Fineman constitute a shared burden across society's institutions.[26] The university is not only an academic institution, but a caregiving one. It is one of these societal entities that is the same time vulnerable as well as a part of the

---

[21]Rider and others (n 16) p 18, IV.B.1.a.
[22]Rider and others (n 16).
[23]Rider and others (n 16) II.A.4.a.
[24]ACGME (n 16).
[25]Fineman (n 3).
[26]Fineman (n 3).

array of social institutions, which includes professional organisations, which promote resilience and social well-being.

Under significant distress, the vulnerability of the university or of professional organisations is not contained. Academics and professionals, as individuals embedded within the university and other societal organisations share in the vulnerability and the resilience of the primary organisation. The goal of resilience for the institution or for the individual is the restoration of a homoeostatic norm at a level that is the same as or better than that which previously existed. To restore this level of function, the response of the university would be varied, but would potentially involve setting new policies, evaluating its investments and income sources and to look at decreasing cash outflow. If the downturn were significant enough, they might stop funding less financially significant or money-losing portions of their services – in other words to consider laying off or furloughing employees (faculty, professionals, staff and support workers). These responses unmask the limited resilience of the vulnerable academic professional.

In order to sustain a social justice mission, academic professionals must seek out grants or failing that must spend their own time and/or money accomplishing projects about which they are passionate. For the university, the best kinds of grants are those federal and rare private grants that come with "indirect cost recovery" or, as it is sometimes referred to, "full cost recovery".[27] This means that in addition to the money to actually do a grant-funded project, the granting agency, usually the federal government, pays an additional amount of money outside the grant-funded dollar value to pay for the support staff salaries and time, space, equipment, and other resources that, while not directly used in the project are essential for the successful completion of the project. Smaller grants, often those from private companies and foundations specifically will not pay for salaries (or salary fringe costs) or for the space, time and resources to accomplish the project. Projects relating to social justice are especially poorly funded and frequently have to be funded out of university or department budgets. Professional organisations similarly have little funding for these social justice projects. In order to accomplish these underfunded or unfunded projects, professionals must use their own time, that is, to take time away from money-earning clinical duties. This time redirection is recognised as necessary but is unpopular with administrators and administrative faculty. In the face of external stressors, the university in order to restore financial balance may increase the target time or clinical output production of healthcare providers, effectively shutting off the potential for unfunded socially relevant projects. Whether the resilience-driven response of the university is to eliminate costs by decreasing salaries and jobs or by increasing the output of the academic professional, the response necessarily unmasks the vulnerability of the faculty, staff and students. This necessitates a resilience response from these entities which may act to decrease the time spent on projects that promote resilience in the community.

The current Covid-19 pandemic offers insight into how the university, in this case Emory University, as a vulnerable entity, responded to a highly unusual and highly stressful situation. The initial response was to ask faculty, staff and students to quarantine and to develop virtual courses to complete the semester. Salaries were paid and administrative support was at first supportive, but as finances grew tighter, various money-cutting and salary-cutting measures were undertaken. The university-directed

[27] <www.tnlcommunityfund.org.uk/funding/funding-guidance/full-cost-recovery> Accessed March 22, 2021.

measures put more time and financial pressure on faculty, staff and related professionals such as to cause the unmasking of the limitations of resilience. Faculty was expected to work from home, to develop their own computer resources to be more involved in their own billings, and to develop zoom conferences for their students. This decreased the need for office space in university buildings, and decreased need for the housekeeping staff that cleaned the buildings. Also decreased was the need for some billing and coding persons, and for university information technology (IT) persons since personal computer equipment was being used which did not require university IT support. These persons could be laid off. Some administrative support was needed, but because the transition to tele-working was in place, fewer of these people were needed as well. They were furloughed or asked to take a cut in pay. Because the schools were closed and children were supposed to be learning virtually, professional parents had to redirect some of their time away from university academics to home-schooling. Day care was also closed and nannies were not available so that in the two professionals household parents had to alternate academic and clinical work with childcare responsibilities. If the clinical role of the parent was on the inpatient side where telemedicine was not possible and physical presence was required, further complications arose. The faculty had to leave their children in some fashion (swapping out duties with the other parent, curtailing clinical time). The university responded in its own best interest, but this caused a wide variety of unforeseen consequences to the academic professional who in turn had to try and stabilise their own situation. In doing so, this caused further downstream stressors for other less well paid staff who were least likely to be able to respond well or fully. In terms of vulnerability theory, the evolution of the Covid-19 pandemic forced each lower level into situations of decreasing potential for resilience. Another unfortunate casualty of the pandemic is that social justice projects that previously had been done in the community could no longer be done. This forced those communities and their members to revert back to when they were less resilient and more subject to life without resources.

Emory initiatives aimed at training professions in social justice

Over the past 12 years one of the authors (WRS) developed several initiatives, projects and courses that aimed at the attitudes, knowledge and skills of our faculty, students and other interested persons. The underlying purpose of these efforts was to train and demonstrate the various ways that the professional can contribute to enhancing resilience for both learners and society.

Emory's Urban Health Initiative (UHI) and the Ethics and Engaged Professionalism Project (E2P2) were developed to collaboratively work across professions to address the issues of educating learners in the knowledge and skills essential to performing social justice as a part of professionalism. These projects focus on advocacy and ethics training of professionals (across a range of professions) at any stage of professional activity, from trainee to seasoned professional.

UHI is a project funded in part by the School of Medicine as well as governmental grants. Significant work is done by student volunteers and faculty professionals who volunteer their time. Since the university funding and grant funding are aimed primarily at administrative support and project completion, much of the work of this project is done because it is the passion of those who volunteer. The UHI is focused on helping under-resourced urban communities address healthcare disparities and the social determinants of health.

The E2P2 project is run out of Emory's Center for Ethics, and is a collaboration between the Center for Ethics, UHI, and five of nine of Emory's academic schools. It is entirely volunteer. Significant training and advocacy occur through this programme. The training occurs in several core areas: (1) policy and legislative advocacy; (2) community engagement; and (3) professional ethics, integrity and leadership; (4) bias, profiling, stigma and discrimination. The project's methodology includes didactic and experiential training to encourage and reinforce ongoing identity formation. While the E2P2 project reinforces the commitment to social justice inherent across the professions, it also reinforces the role of the professional in generating positive change (resilience) individually and in communities. For the past three years we have run a three-semester hour course out of Emory's Laney Graduate School. Currently we are in the process of developing each of the experiential tracks into a programme through which a certificate can be earned. E2P2 has addressed the issue of developing "engaged professionals" by considering the societal expectations of the professional and teaching both developing as well as active professionals. The E2P2 project offers a non-required, but widely sought-after curriculum that focuses on professional obligations as they relate to social justice and the promotion of patient/client/customer well-being. The project demonstrates how the developing professional can effectively work with communities in its core areas of focus.

If the efforts of UHI and E2P2 and other similar projects are to make an impact, professional schools must look beyond the oft-cited "tripartite" academic mission of healthcare training (clinical, education and research). A fourth mission of the modern professional school must be advocacy (or social justice). It is only by recognising the importance of adding – and supporting – this fourth mission that a professional school can truly demonstrate commitment to society. The vision of the E2P2 project is that, "All professionals will engage collaboratively to improve their communities and the lives of those who live there."[28] The project trains and mentors learners and active professionals in developing the "values, knowledge, and skills necessary to serve in leading positive and collaborative change within the communities where they work and live".[29] The objective of E2P2 is to arm the engaged professional with the experience and training essential for meaningful community engagement. The project has begun the development of web-based training modules.

As we have worked in the community, it has become obvious that aspiring to equality or even equity in trying to facilitate resilience is insufficient. Only through providing opportunity in addition to equity can community members (and communities) gain sufficient strength to become truly resilient. Examples of this kind of opportunity are evident in the "Young Entrepreneur's Project" (which teaches high school students how to make garden-related projects, to market and sell them, and to save the money so it will not be stolen in a high-risk part of the city); the "Seniors Project" (which has medical students interacting with low-income seniors, and where the students teach the seniors about health and the seniors teach the students about indigent neighbourhoods); and the "Food as Medicine" Prescription Project (where mock prescriptions for healthy food are given by students and physicians to low-

[28]W Sexson, "E2P2 Strategic Plan" (file document, 2018).
[29]Fineman (n 3).

resourced inner-city people to help them purchase healthy choices in food). These example projects were completed at the Emory Urban Health Initiative's Community Garden, which is placed in an extremely resource-depleted area and "food desert" within the city of Atlanta. All of these projects stem from Emory University social justice initiatives which focus on the social determinants of health and deal with community and individual resilience. A companion article in this publication ("The Positive and Negative Roles of Grant Funding as Mechanisms for Societal Transformation and the Development of Community Resilience") was presented in October 2019 as part of the Nottingham conference on "Vulnerability and the Organisation of Academic Labour". This presentation and the paper detail the conduct and consequences – sometimes good, sometimes unfortunate – of community-based research.[30]

Recommendations

Stemming from the Charter on Professionalism, if the principles and commitments outlined above are deeply considered, one sees a set of guidelines that could be adopted broadly across all professions. The commitments relating to the professional's responsibility to individuals and to society are especially important when considering societal resilience. A set of inter-professionally created, professionalism-based principles and commitment might be developed into a working structure where a profession (broadly defined) and the individual professional would act to facilitate resilience and social justice.

The recommendations below address the general obligations of professional schools. These recommendations are based on the literature noted above and target the development of resilience within our communities and society generally. Specifically,

- Professional schools should affirm that advocacy is a legitimate focus beyond the traditional academic pillars of clinical, education, and research. In order to affirm this commitment, professional schools should commit money and support promotion in faculty whose focus is in community-engaged or societal advocacy.
- Interprofessional academic entities, such as the E2P2 project, should be recognised and encouraged as essential to providing education to faculty and trainees of various professional schools.
- Consideration should be given to the development of an intra-national or international set of interprofessionally created, professionalism-based principles and commitments (similar to the Charter on Professionalism, noted above) which provide a working structure for the promotion of professionalism. This could be a further outcome of the October 2019 conference.

Conclusion

The claim that this paper makes is that the university and the academic professional, through the lens of "engaged professionalism", can contribute to the development of

---

[30] J Wilson and W Sexson, "The Positive and Negative Roles of Grant Funding as Mechanisms for Societal Transformation and the Development of Community Resilience" (Paper presentation, Vulnerability and the Organisation of Academic Labour Conference, October 2019).

resilience in society. By reinforcing the importance of societal advocacy as well as interprofessional projects such as E2P2, engaged members of the professions can contribute significantly to the realisation of the individual and societal resilience that is the counter to universal vulnerability.

Legal education has a crucial role to play in this enterprise. As Twining argued, legal education needs to open up to other professions and to society.[31] Consideration of what justice entails is important beyond legal academia. In our teaching,[32] in our research,[33] and in our contributions to public discourse,[34] academics who teach professionalism can make a real contribution to our collective future resilience.

Disclosure statement

No potential conflict of interest was reported by the authors.

[31]William Twining, "Rethinking Legal Education" (2018) 52 The Law Teacher 241.

[32]Nicola Harris, Roxanna Dehaghani and Daniel Newman, "Vulnerability, the Future of the Criminal Defence Profession, and the Implications for Teaching and Learning" this issue of The Law Teacher.

[33]Joan Wilson and WR Sexson, "The Positive and Negative Roles of Grant Funding as Mechanisms for Societal Transformation and the Development of Community Resilience", this issue of The Law Teacher.

[34]Fabrizia Serafim, "Vulnerability Theory as a Tool against a Banking Model of Legal Education", this issue of The Law Teacher.

Index